Crafting
Common Worship

A practical, creative guide to what's possible

Peter Moger

with case studies by

Tim Lomax

and contributions from

Ally Barrett, Paul Bayes, Peter Craig-Wild, Kate Lomax, Anne Lowen, Lucy Moore, Tim Stratford and Carl Turner

 CHURCH HOUSE PUBLISHING

Church House Publishing
Church House
Great Smith Street
London SW1P 3AZ

Tel: 020 7898 1451
Fax: 020 7898 1449

ISBN 978–0–7151–4201–1

Published 2009 by Church House Publishing

Typeset in 10pt Optima and Gill Sans
by RefineCatch Limited, Bungay, Suffolk
Printed in the UK by CPI William Clowes Beccles NR34 7TL

Contents

Foreword

Somewhere, every day of most weeks, a priest of the Church of England will hear read the *Declaration of Assent* and be asked to affirm its contents. In this affirmation a slightly ominous note is struck at the point where they must declare that they 'will use only the forms of service which are authorized or allowed by Canon'. The declaration that they will have heard read, however, is couched in far more positive terms. Indeed, it is a masterpiece of prose, summarizing that which needs to be affirmed by all clergy and any who are responsible for leading or 'crafting' worship. The preface takes us to the heart of the declaration:

> Led by the Holy Spirit, [the Church of England] has borne witness to Christian truth in its historic formularies, the Thirty-Nine Articles of Religion, *The Book of Common Prayer*, and the Ordering of Bishops, Priests and Deacons.

Putting on one side the Articles, all else that is mentioned is worship. This reminds us that the Church of England expresses its belief almost entirely through worship and prayer. This is why the project aimed at providing contemporary texts and resources for worship is itself titled *Common Worship*. The aim of *Common Worship* is to preserve that sense of our corporate life being fashioned by prayer and the liturgy. At the same time *Common Worship* allows sufficient flexibility and scope for creativity so that the great variety of occasions, styles and needs in worship might be served while using resources that are still held in common.

This book shows how this process, rooted in a positive 'creative tension', may be pursued with imagination but also with an eye to the common tradition which shapes the nature of Anglicanism. It offers clergy and worship committees alike the resources they need and includes helpful 'exemplary material'. The appendices gather together those formal canons, rubrics and guidelines which hold this process together. Peter Moger, the Church of England's National Worship Development Officer, and his team are to be congratulated on their balance and creativity. As Chair of the Liturgical Commission I commend this book most warmly.

† Stephen Wakefield

Acknowledgements

I should like to express my gratitude to all who have helped make this book a reality:

- Mark Pilgrim and Bristol Diocesan Liturgical Committee, for 'starting the ball rolling' by inviting me to contribute workshops on 'law and freedom in *Common Worship*' to the 2008 Diocesan Clergy Conference
- Tim Lomax, who deserves special recognition for assembling many of the case studies and reading and commenting on the text at various stages along the way
- The members of the Liturgical Commission and others who have willingly supplied material for inclusion
- Colleagues at Church House: in particular Colin Podmore for his thorough reading of the text and helpful comments, Kathryn Pritchard for her enthusiastic engagement with the project and editorial guidance, and Linda Foster, for her meticulous attention to detail.

Finally, thanks are due to my wife, Heather, and my sons Thomas and David, for their encouragement and forbearance at those times when I have been rather more preoccupied than usual.

Peter Moger

July 2009

Introduction

This is a book for anyone who plans or leads worship in the Church of England. Clergy, Readers and lay worship leaders all play a crucial part in helping people, day by day and week by week, to draw near to God in praise and prayer and be transformed by their encounter with him. Worship really matters! It is, after all, the primary activity of the Christian Church.

The book has grown out of my work as National Worship Development Officer – a post created by the Church of England in 2005 to promote good practice in the preparation and leading of worship, particularly following the completion of the *Common Worship* enterprise. As I have travelled around the dioceses during the past three years, two things have become very clear:

- Significant numbers of people who lead worship are unaware of all that *Common Worship* offers.
- They are usually even less sure about how to use it all!

This isn't surprising, because *Common Worship* isn't really like anything the church has known before. We've moved from having a service book (or books) to having a vast collection of structures and resources for worship. *Common Worship* is a radical departure for the Church of England – radical in that it goes back to the *roots* of what worship is and how it works, which is:

- that worship carries each of us on a journey;
- that there is an expectation that as we worship we shall meet God face to face;
- that, through this encounter, we shall be changed; and
- that our worship leads to mission.

The context in which we worship and minister is also not like anything we've known before. We are – praise God – part of a church which is rediscovering its missionary identity. Recent developments, across all traditions, are both exciting and challenging. But, as the report *Transforming Worship* reminds us, 'If the Church is truly to realize its calling to share in God's mission in the world, then its members need to be formed by worship.'[1] *Common Worship* is designed to give churches and ministers both the permission and the resources to create worship to enable that formation to take place.

Crafting Common Worship opens our eyes to the vast store-cupboard of ingredients at our disposal, and looks at ways in which those ingredients may be combined to create dishes which will nourish and sustain God's people in worship.

We begin by asking 'What's new about *Common Worship*?' We tackle the thorny question of what it means for licensed ministers to promise to obey the law concerning worship. Then we look at the structures *Common Worship* provides and how, like Ezekiel's bones, they can be infused with life.

This isn't a book about liturgical theory, but worshipping practice. And so the final three chapters consist of case studies showing how ministers in a variety of contexts have used *Common Worship* to create acts of worship which are engaging and mission-focused.

Abbreviations

Liturgy

BCP	*The Book of Common Prayer*
CW	*Common Worship*
CWCI	*Common Worship: Christian Initiation* (CHP, 2006)
CWCPC	*Common Worship: Collects and Post Communions* (CHP, 2004)
CWDP	*Common Worship: Daily Prayer* (CHP, 2005)
CWF	*Common Worship: Festivals* (CHP, 2008)
CWMV	*Common Worship: Services and Prayers for the Church of England* (CHP, 2000)
CWOrd	*Common Worship: Ordination Services* (CHP, 2007)
CWPE	*Common Worship: President's Edition* (CHP, 2000)
CWPS	*Common Worship: Pastoral Services* (CHP, 2000, 2nd edn 2005)
CWT&S	*Common Worship: Times and Seasons* (CHP, 2006)
NPFW	*New Patterns for Worship* (2002, 2nd edn 2008)

Music

CAHON	*Hymns Old and New (Complete Anglican Edition)*, Kevin Mayhew, 2000
CG	*Common Ground* (St Andrew Press, 1998)
CH4	*The Church Hymnary, fourth edition* (Canterbury Press, 2007) – also published as *Hymns of Glory, Songs of Praise* (Canterbury Press, 2008)
CMP	*Complete Mission Praise* (Marshall Pickering / HarperCollins 1999, expanded edition, 2005)
CP	*Common Praise* (Canterbury Press, 2000)
SG	*Sing Glory* (Jubilate Hymns / Kevin Mayhew, 1999)
SOF	*Songs of Fellowship* (Kingsway, 1991–2007)
TS	*The Source* (Kevin Mayhew, 1998–2005)

1

Common Worship: A new way of doing liturgy?

Diversity in worship today

If we were able to walk into an English parish church at 11 a.m. on a Sunday morning in 1959 – most of us would get something of a shock. For one thing, the service would probably have been non-eucharistic (at least if the church was of 'low' or 'central' tradition): Matins from *The Book of Common Prayer*. Holy Communion would have been celebrated earlier, at 8 a.m. There would have been hymns (but not worship songs), and the psalms and canticles would have been sung by choir and congregation to Anglican chant. The language, with the exception of the sermon, would have been that of the sixteenth and seventeenth centuries. The service would have been led, almost exclusively, by the (male) priest. The congregation would have sat to listen, stood to sing and knelt to pray, but always within the confines of their pews.

A lot has changed in the last 50 years, so moving the clock forward to a present-day service, we are struck by the host of differences between the two acts of worship. The most significant difference, though, is that if one turns up at a parish church at random, it is hard to predict exactly what will be on the liturgical menu. There is a strong probability that the main service on a Sunday morning will be eucharistic (whatever the tradition of the church) and that the service will be in contemporary language, but other than that the possibilities of variety are considerable. It may be an all-age service, or it may involve the use of projected images and movement around the building. It's quite likely that the music will encompass a range of styles and could be led by an informal group of singers and instrumentalists, or by a robed choir, or there might even not be any music at all. Those involved in leading parts of the worship may be lay or ordained, male or female.

We now have immense variety in our worship, both between one church and the next and also *within* churches. And so it's not so unusual to find a church where the Sunday diet might look something like this:

8.00	Holy Communion (BCP)
9.30	Parish Eucharist (*Common Worship* Order 1)
11.15	Parish Praise

6.00	Evening Prayer (*Common Worship*) / Evensong (BCP) / Taizé worship / Healing service – depending on the Sunday of the month
8.00	(monthly) 'The late service'

And of course all kinds of other things might happen during the week, on- or off-site, as a 'fresh expression'.

We've travelled a vast distance during the past 50 years, and the rate of change has been increasing all the time. In terms of our worship, we are becoming a self-consciously 'mixed-economy' church. As the Archbishop of Canterbury, Dr Rowan Williams, has written, 'there's no one kind of church life that captures everything, that does every kind of job.'[2] One of the most encouraging developments within the Church of England in recent years (across all traditions) is the increasing focus on mission, and a growing realization that there is a vital link between mission and worship. It's a link that works two ways. On the one hand we need forms of worship which are sufficiently accessible to the de-churched and unchurched. On the other, we need engaging, transformative worship which holds, nurtures and challenges those who are growing in their faith.

We have realized that, where worship is concerned, 'one size will not fit all' and that to serve up a uniform diet is to fail to provide for people at different stages of their faith journey and with differing personality types and learning styles. While BCP Evensong is increasing in popularity, especially in cathedrals, it is now true that Matins is no longer the default setting for Anglican morning worship. Within a broad and diverse church such as ours we need variety.

So in this opening chapter we will begin to lift the lid on *Common Worship* which, together with *The Book of Common Prayer*, provides the liturgical texts for Church of England worship. We shall cover briefly the background to *Common Worship* – the period leading up to its creation – and then move to an overview of its contents, before asking the important question 'What's different about *Common Worship*?' Finally we shall look at the place that liturgical structure occupies within it.

The background to *Common Worship*: A time of revision

The 50 years between 1959 and 2009 saw an immense amount of activity in the field of liturgical revision, both within the Church of England and ecumenically. From a situation in 1959 where *The Book of Common Prayer* was the only authorized text for Church of England worship, we have moved through successive waves of revised and new texts.

The 1960s and 1970s brought us Alternative Services: Series 1, 2 and 3.[3] While the services of Series 1 moved little beyond the changes of the proposed *Prayer Book* of 1928, those in Series 2 and 3 broke significant new ground. Services began to mirror developments in structure and text taking place in other Christian churches and (in Series 3) for the first time, contemporary language broke onto the liturgical scene: God, hitherto addressed as 'thou' became 'you'.

The Alternative Services led to the *Alternative Service Book 1980*, authorized initially for ten years and subsequently for a further ten. They drew together the revisions of the previous two decades. Hard on the heels of the ASB came a book of pastoral resources, *Ministry to the Sick* (1983) and two seasonal books, *Lent, Holy Week, Easter* (1986) and *The Promise of His Glory* (1991) which introduced the joys of seasonal worship to parts of the Church which had never previously experienced them. Further new material arrived in 1995 in the shape of *Patterns for Worship*, published shortly after newly authorized provision in *A Service of the Word*. With the authorization of the ASB due to end at the millennium, the wholesale revision of the Church of England's liturgy was now in full spate.

Common Worship

Following some initial volumes in 1997 and 1998 (*Calendar, Lectionary and Collects* and an interim edition of *Initiation Services*), *Common Worship: Services and Prayers for the Church of England* was published in 2000, and authorized for use from Advent Sunday of that year.

The publication of *Common Worship* took eight years and spans nine principal volumes – the final volume appearing on the shelves in February 2008 – but represents many more years of creative work: of drafting, experimental use, debate in the General Synod and the House of Bishops, and painstaking revision.

Common Worship: The complete collection

Before starting to delve in detail into the resources contained within *Common Worship*, it's good to remind ourselves what all the volumes are and get an overview of what they include.

Common Worship: Services and Prayers for the Church of England (2000) (CWMV)

This volume – usually referred to as the 'main volume' includes a range of 'mainstream' services which might be used in Sunday worship: Morning, Evening and Night Prayer, A Service of the Word, Holy Communion, Thanksgiving for the Gift of a Child, Holy Baptism, together with creeds and affirmations of faith, the Psalter, collects and various prayers.

Common Worship: President's Edition (2000) (CWPE)

Much of what is in the main volume is also included here, but in a large format; this is a book designed for use by those presiding at Holy Communion. The *President's Edition* also contains material not in the main volume (e.g. additional eucharistic prefaces and other presidential texts, and also music for the eucharistic prayers).

Common Worship: Pastoral Services (2000, 2nd edn 2005) (CWPS)

The Pastoral Services volume includes services and material to resource wholeness and healing, marriage and funeral ministry. The second edition also includes the 'traditional language' Burial and Holy Matrimony services from Alternative Services: Series 1, based on those in the 1928 *Prayer Book*.

Common Worship: Collects and Post Communions (2004) (CWCPC)

This book contains both the original *Common Worship* collects and post communions and the additional collects (2004) alongside one another. It replaces an earlier interim volume from 1997.

Common Worship: Daily Prayer (2005) (CWDP)

This is a comprehensive resource for daily prayer which includes orders for Morning, Evening and Night Prayer and Prayer During the Day throughout the year, together with collects, canticles, the Psalter and forms of intercession.

Common Worship: Christian Initiation (2006) (CWCI)

This definitive edition of *Christian Initiation* (which replaces an earlier interim volume from 1998) includes all initiation services (including Baptism and Confirmation) together with Rites on the Way: Approaching Baptism, Rites of Affirmation: Appropriating Baptism and Reconciliation and Restoration: Recovering Baptism.

Common Worship: Times and Seasons (2006) (CWT&S)

This volume includes material (service outlines, fully worked-out services and resources) for the two cycles of seasonal time within the Christian Year, from Advent to Candlemas and from Lent to Pentecost, for the festivals and seasons of the agricultural year, for Trinity Sunday, Bible Sunday, Dedication Festival and the period between All Saints' Day and Advent.

Common Worship: Ordination Services (2007) (CWOrd)

This study edition includes the *Common Worship* services for the ordination of deacons, priests and bishops, together with the 1662 Ordinal, and supporting introductory, historical and explanatory material, together with practical guidance.

Common Worship: Festivals (2008) (CWF)

This is a volume designed for the president at Holy Communion and includes resources for the celebration of Festivals, Lesser Festivals, the Common of the Saints and special occasions. The text of Holy Communion Order One is also included, as is music for the eucharistic prayers.

During the same period of time, the Church also published *New Patterns for Worship* (2002, 2nd edn 2008) (NPFW). This is a revision of the 1995 book *Patterns for Worship* and, although not technically part of the body of *Common Worship*, is a complementary resource, set out in 'directory' format (see page 27), with a limited range of sample services. A significant and helpful feature of the book is the inclusion of almost 50 pages of guidance on planning worship.

   In each *Common Worship* volume, the contents pages give a clear overview of what is contained within it. For those whose minds prefer to work with diagrams, a helpful tool is Phillip Tovey's booklet *Mapping Common Worship*.[4] This presents a summary of the contents of each volume in the form of a mind map, with page numbers to aid quick location of material.

So what's different about *Common Worship*?

When the first volumes appeared in 2000, not everyone realized the quantum shift that had taken place. Despite some similarities with what had gone before, CW was not simply a revision of older material.

   There were those who, in 2000, declared 'CW won't affect us' and went on to make their services as close to those in the ASB as they could. But they had totally missed the point. CW enshrines a new concept for a new era. Whereas the ASB reads very much as a product of the modern age, CW is more a product of post-modernity. This is visible in a number of ways.

1. Multiple media

CW is much more than simply a library of books. The texts of CW are published in three ways, and in a variety of media:

   a. in printed form;
   b. electronically, on the Church of England's web site;[5]
   c. as part of the *Visual Liturgy* worship-planning software.[6]

While the printed texts are widely used for reference, a great many people prefer to use the electronic versions for preparing service booklets and sheets or PowerPoint slides. With the advent of *Common Worship*, many churches decided to move away from having a 'service book' to using a series of locally produced seasonal booklets for their worship. Some opted to create one-off sheets for each service, and others have gone down the 'paperless' road of projecting liturgical texts onto a screen. The fact is that we now inhabit a 'download, cut and paste' culture, in which choice, selection and the availability of a range of options are the norm.

2. Designed for a 'mixed-economy' church

The possibility of 'cutting and pasting' from within *Common Worship* means that it is a resource designed to serve a church in which worship flourishes across a range of traditions and in an ever-growing variety of situations. As the Preface to *Common Worship* puts it, 'The services provided here are rich and varied. This reflects the multiplicity of contexts in which worship is offered today.'[7] Given the rate of change in much of the church's worship, it is inevitable that many of the contexts in which worship is offered in 2009 were not necessarily envisaged in 2000. Developments such as the flourishing of fresh expressions has in some cases led to a robust dialogue between those who wish to push the frontiers of Anglican liturgical expression and those who wish to maintain the status quo. Nevertheless, the intention of CW is that it should serve the 'mixed economy' church which we inhabit – a church which balances Evangelical and Catholic insights, liberal and conservative emphases, and traditional and fresh expressions of church.

3. Something old, something new

Another important concept in CW comes out of the realization that we now inhabit a post-modern culture in which old and new exist side by side. The ASB was, by and large, a contemporary language 'alternative' to set alongside the traditional language of the BCP. This led to more than a degree of polarization. The formation of the Prayer Book Society in 1972 grew out of concerns that, in jumping on the bandwagon of liturgical progress, the Church was in serious danger of leaving behind a body of liturgy which had nourished – and was still nourishing – generations of Anglicans.

In the run-up to CW, the Liturgical Commission was anxious to engage with advocates of traditional language. This was reflected in the appointment of the novelist Baroness James of Holland Park, a Vice-President of the Prayer Book Society, as a member of the Commission from 1991. And when CW was produced, a conscious decision was taken that it should include 'treasures both old and new'. There are two orders for Holy Communion, each of them in modern and traditional language, with one of those traditional options being the Prayer Book service as it is celebrated today.

BCP Matins and Evensong, and Night Prayer using the texts from 1928 Compline are included, as are the collects in traditional language. The second edition of the *Pastoral Services* volume (2005) also includes the Series 1 (traditional language) marriage and burial services, both of which stand firmly in the BCP tradition.

But what is perhaps most significant is that in CW no intentional wedge is driven between the old and the new. And so it is now quite possible to move between the two within the context of a single act of worship (see the Case Study: 'Prayer Book Evensong revisited' on page 73). This is not to deny the importance of liturgical linguistic integrity, but to recognize the variety of our culture and enable that to be expressed within our worship. The phrase 'ancient-future worship' was scarcely known in 2000 but CW in a sense anticipates a trend for worship in which the contemporary and the time-honoured sit cheek by jowl.

So *Common Worship* is quite different from what came before: with traditional and new material side by side, published in several forms, it is designed to serve the mixed-economy church of today. But what would Archbishop Cranmer have made of it?

Common Worship, common prayer and structure

Thomas Cranmer's aim was to provide a single liturgical use for the whole of England:

> And whereas heretofore there hath been great diversity in saying and singing in Churches within this Realm; some following *Salisbury* Use, some *Hereford* Use, and some the Use of *Bangor*, some of *York*, some of *Lincoln*; now from henceforth all the whole Realm shall have but one Use. (*Concerning the Service of the Church* from *The Book of Common Prayer*, 1549)

This was very much a product of his time. The invention of the printing press by William Caxton in 1476 meant that, for the first time in history, multiple copies of a single text could be produced economically and quickly. And so Cranmer's *Book of Common Prayer* was able, through its text, to bring about a culture of 'common prayer' throughout the whole Church. With the exception of the Commonwealth years, *The Books of Common Prayer* (in their various editions) continued to do this until the Alternative Services of the 1960s and 1970s. While Anglicans might have differed in their theological stances and liturgical practices, they did nevertheless all pray the same words.

The BCP is a book of services, which reads continuously and – apart from a very few options (e.g. a choice from two post communion prayers, selections of Scripture sentences and a handful of Proper Prefaces) – without variation. It's possible to pick up a BCP, start at the beginning of a service and read it to the end (though of course, in the case of Prayer Book Holy

Communion, virtually no one does!). Despite having been written four centuries later, the ASB was not a million miles culturally from the world of the BCP. The language was (largely) modern, and some variation was permitted (e.g. in the provision of a range of eucharistic prayers and some seasonal texts) but it was still a book in which the services read continuously. Many of us will remember all too well that Holy Communion Rite A began on page 119 of the ASB! This perpetuated a sense of 'common prayer' through the text of the service: the same words being prayed in churches across the land. The run-up to CW saw changes in the understanding of 'common prayer' in the Church of England. A crucial publication was *The Renewal of Common Prayer: Unity and Diversity in Church of England Worship.*[8] In this collection of essays, members of the Liturgical Commission discussed what 'common prayer' might mean in the light of growing freedom and variety in worship. In particular, the writers argued a rationale for a common prayer rooted less in liturgical text than in liturgical structure. Michael Vasey wrote, 'It has been an important insight of modern liturgical study that it is shape rather than particular texts that provide the common core, the "deep structure", of the major acts of Christian worship.'[9] The authorization by the General Synod in 1993 of *A Service of the Word* gave a clear signal that it was in this direction that the future of common prayer was to lie.

And so, in CW, it is, above all, *structure* which acts as the unifying factor across the entire range of material, together with the common use of certain key texts. All CW services have what has been called a 'family likeness' – a similarity of structure, whatever text they might contain. This structure is basically fourfold and is designed to take us on a journey. It reinforces the important point that through taking part in worship we are changed: as we gather, engage with God, respond to him, and are sent to live as his people in the world. With repetition, this structure can become embedded in the psyche and can become a powerful formative influence on the lives of Christians. Just imagine a situation where all Anglicans came to church

- expecting to meet God;
- expecting to be changed by the encounter; and
- expecting to be sent out to do something about it!

Although the titles of the structural blocks vary slightly from service to service, the general pattern throughout the whole of CW is as follows:

- **We gather . . .**
  . . . as the people of God and prepare to meet with him
- **We hear God's word . . .**
  . . . through the reading of the Scriptures
- **We respond . . .**
  . . . to that engagement through some kind of action, e.g.
  o sharing in a celebration of the Eucharist

o baptizing
o commending a dead person
o praying
o marrying
o ordaining
• **We are sent out . . .**
. . . to live the gospel as changed people.

This fourfold structure reflects two basic underlying theological concepts:
in Christ

- God shares our life (the doctrine of incarnation);
- and transforms it (the doctrine or redemption).

And so, by taking part in worship with this structure – in journeying through
the structure – the potential is there for us to be formed into a particular
understanding of how God interacts with us.

But does common prayer really matter? It could be argued that it is an idea
which has had its day and no longer has any place within the brave new
world of a mixed-economy, post-modern church. Traditionally, Anglicans
believe that common prayer *does* matter, and is vitally important, for two
reasons.

1. It is through our worship that we have traditionally done our theology
   and expressed our identity (see Chapter 2).
2. Although the local church is a crucial part of our life, we are also part
   of something much bigger. A sense of common prayer reinforces our
   belief as Anglicans in the catholicity of the Church: that the local is a
   part of, and relates to, the whole. The fourfold structure which
   undergirds *Common Worship* is a feature which is common to
   virtually all revised liturgies of the mainstream churches.

In recent years, some local churches within the Church of England have
chosen to distance themselves from this structural pattern, and have followed
what has in many places become a new standard form of 'praise, preaching
and prayer ministry'. In so doing, they are in danger losing touch not only
with their ecclesial roots, but also with the essential theological premises
which underpin the structure. There is also the potential risk that, without
continual reference to the essential elements of the structure of worship,
some important elements might be lacking. I heard recently of a large
Anglican church where, at the main Sunday service, although there was
preaching and prayer ministry, no intercessory prayer was offered for the
world beyond the church, and the only reading from Scripture was of a single
verse from the Old Testament.

Common Worship then, does represent a new way of doing liturgy.
Although it has been with us almost nine years, it has taken that long for

many people to realize how different it is to what has gone before. It represents a serious attempt to hold two things in creative tension: on the one hand, recognizably Anglican forms of worship, and on the other, provision for diversity. The success of *Common Worship* will depend to a large extent on the willingness of ministers to engage with it: to absorb the frameworks and deep structures and to interpret and articulate them in fresh and engaging ways within their local churches, making best use of the flexibility and freedom it encourages.

The writer of Ecclesiastes wrote: 'Of the making of books there is no end' (Ecclesiastes 12.12b.) To some, it might seem that he was writing about *Common Worship*! In *Common Worship*, we have a large resource, but it should be a priority for all who plan and lead worship to be familiar with its contents. There is no real substitute for spending time exploring each of the volumes and discovering what lies within them. While the electronic provision of texts has made the selection of appropriate texts very much easier than ever before, it has meant that we are often less familiar with the contents of the books than we might have been in times past. And because of that, we might also be unaware of some of the material within them or of their creative possibilities.

But how do flexibility and freedom fit within a church whose ministers take an oath of obedience to their bishop, and promise to keep the law – especially in relation to worship? The next chapter looks at the law concerning public worship:

- why it matters;
- what it says; and
- whether it is about policing or enabling creativity.

2

'. . . authorized or allowed by Canon'

The church was packed: parishioners, family, friends, well-wishers from previous places of ministry had all gathered to support Jane as she was instituted as the new Vicar of St Mark's. The opening hymn was sung, the bishop greeted the congregation and the patron made his presentation. Then the bishop pronounced: 'Let the Declaration of Assent be made and subscribed and the Oaths taken according to law.' Jane declared her belief in the faith revealed in the Holy Scriptures, and ended '. . . I will use only the forms of service which are authorized or allowed by Canon.'

Those of us who are licensed ministers might sometimes have wondered about the wisdom of having made that Declaration.

- Perhaps because we know there could be times when we might use forms of worship which are not authorized or allowed by canon.
- Perhaps because, with Mr Bumble in *Oliver Twist*,[10] we simply think that 'the law is a ass' (*sic*).
- Perhaps because we don't really know what *is* authorized or allowed by canon, and might think differently if we did.

Anglican identity and worship

In other words, it is to the texts used in its worship (and in particular those from *The Book of Common Prayer* and the Ordinal) that the Church of England looks to give expression to its theology.

Anglicans have traditionally expressed their identity and done their theology through their worship. As the Preface to *Common Worship* puts it (CWMV, page ix): 'The forms of worship authorized in the Church of England express our faith and help to create our identity.' Unlike those churches which adhere to confessional statements (whether the *Catechism of the Catholic Church* or the *Augsburg Confession*), the Church of England has preferred to say: 'if you want to know what Anglicans believe, then worship with us and find out.'[11] It is for this reason that public worship in the Church of England is a matter governed by law, and that, in making the Declaration of Assent, the minister promises that:

> . . . in public prayer and administration of the sacraments, I will
> use only the forms of service which are authorized or allowed
> by Canon.

Before we go on to look at what the canons say about worship, it's worth
remembering two things about what ministers promise in the Declaration
of Assent:

1. The promise refers to 'public worship and the administration of the
   sacraments', in other words to what we do in the public arena, but not
   to our private prayers and devotions, or to worship conducted within
   a 'domestic' setting, such as within a home group.
2. The promise is to use material 'authorized *or allowed*' by canon. It
   is not simply a promise to use *authorized* texts, which are far fewer in
   number than those which are commended or allowed under canon.
   Nor is the authorized material confined to texts, but also – under
   Common Worship – encompasses some authorized structures for
   worship (see Chapter 4).

The Canons which govern worship

For most of us, the Canon Law of the Church of England is not a common
subject of conversation in the local coffee shop, but we can't get away from the
fact that the life of our Church is underpinned by this complex and carefully-
worded collection of laws. Although in their present form the Canons were
written in the 1960s or more recently, many of them embody the ancient
Canon Law of the Church – in some cases going back to the early
Christian Councils and in others to the Middle Ages or the early seventeenth
century.

If we are to make the best, and most creative, use of the resources in
Common Worship, it's vital that we know what the canons say about
worship, and what they mean.

Within the canons,[12] those in Section B relate to public worship and,
within that section there are five which deal with liturgy: Canons B 1 to B 5.
These are printed in full in Appendix 1 (page 148) and – as part of the full
set – are also available to download, free of charge, from the Church of
England web site.[13]

Canon B 1 sets out the general principles of 'conformity of worship' and
lists the various categories of liturgical authorization which are then
expanded upon in Canons B 2 to B 5. Also within Canon B 1 is a reminder
that ministers should 'have a good understanding of the forms of service
used' and that worship offered should both 'glorify God and edify the
people'. In other words, the canons themselves point to the responsibility of
ministers to know the liturgical provision for our Church's worship and how
that liturgy works.

Canon B 2 provides for the General Synod of the Church of England to approve forms of service either with or without time limit. Services approved in this way are alternative to those in the BCP.

Canon B 3 sets out the issues around decisions as to which forms of service should be used.

Canon B 4 enables the convocations, the archbishops in their provinces (of Canterbury and York) or the bishops in their dioceses to approve forms of service for use on occasions where there is neither any provision in the BCP nor in any other authorized alternative services. Examples which fall within this category include An Order of Service for Remembrance Day,[14] which is authorized by the archbishops for use in the Provinces of Canterbury and York, and the diocesan orders for Institution, Induction and Licensing, which are authorized locally by diocesan bishops.

Canon B 5 (paragraph 2) allows discretion to a 'minister having the cure of souls' (i.e. an incumbent or priest-in-charge, or their equivalent in a non-parochial context), where no other provision has been made under Canons B 1 or B 4, to use 'other forms of service that are considered suitable'. Examples of this might include a Christingle or carol service, a commemorative or civic service or other act of worship for the local community. If anyone questions the suitability of such forms of service, then the final decision rests with the bishop. Canon B 5 also allows any minister officiating at a service, at his/her discretion, to make variations which are 'not of substantial importance' to the service. In doing this, a minister has to ensure that any variations are 'reverent and seemly' and that they are in line with the doctrine of the Church of England (Canon B 5.3).

Canon B 5, then, allows considerable freedom – often more than is realized – to the local minister. The nature of this freedom will be discussed more fully in Chapters 3 and 4.

Well, that's all very well, you might say – and you might even have read dutifully through all five canons in the Appendix – but how does this work out in terms of real live worship? And what are 'authorized services'? This is something that can confuse even the most seasoned minister.

Authorized and commended

Throughout the canons, reference is often made to 'authorized' forms of service. In fact, the Church of England has two categories of liturgical text.

1. Authorized Alternative Services

These are services approved by the General Synod under Canon B 2. They are alternative to material in *The Book of Common Prayer*. In other words, if a text is in the BCP and a new, alternative form is proposed, it requires full Synodical authorization. This can be a lengthy process – as is only right when our liturgical texts carry the weight of the Church of England's doctrine. The authorization of a new text by the General Synod takes place only after considerable discussion, revision and debate.

- Examples of authorized texts include
  - The Orders for Holy Communion
  - Eucharistic Prayers
  - Creeds and Affirmations of Faith
  - Forms of Confession and Absolution
  - The texts of the Lord's Prayer
  - The Baptism services
  - The Ordination of Deacons, Priests and Bishops
  - The Marriage Service
  - The Funeral Service

Because the BCP remains the liturgical touchstone of Church of England doctrine, it's vital that authorized alternative texts are used without variation. For example, priests don't have the right under Canon Law to compose their own eucharistic prayers (though see below, pages 15 and 60, about prefaces), or to write new creeds or import affirmations of faith from outside the Church of England. These texts – as authorized alternatives to those in the BCP – are expressive of essential doctrine.

2. Commended Services

These are services or texts which the House of Bishops has judged to be suitable either for their own approval under Canon B 4 or for use in the contexts in which ministers draw up their own orders for worship under Canon B 5. They are texts for which there is no comparable material in the BCP, and so while they are fully congruent with Anglican doctrine, they don't bear the same weight as do the authorized texts. Hence, there is a degree of flexibility in the way in which a minister may approach them. For example, a commended text may be shortened, expanded or varied slightly, if a minister sees fit.

Amongst the commended texts are:

- Much of the material in
  - *New Patterns for Worship*
  - *Common Worship: Times and Seasons*
  - *Common Worship: Festivals;*
- The *Rites on the Way* resources in *Common Worship: Christian Initiation;*
- Those contents of *Common Worship: Daily Prayer* which are not alternative to material in the BCP;
- The form for the Admission of the Baptized to Communion;
- Ministry at the Time of Death.

A full list of all the Church of England's authorized and commended worship material is given in Appendix 2 on page 154.

What about material from other provinces and churches?

The world we inhabit enjoys an embarrassment of riches when it comes to worship resources. Never before have there been so many and such varied creative ideas for worship, both in print and online. Many of these are of excellent quality and ministers wanting to lead engaging worship will be keen to make best use of them. But which are authorized for Church of England use?

One question I am often asked is 'Am I allowed to use material from other Anglican provinces?' 'After all,' the reasoning goes, 'they are all part of the Anglican Communion and we all believe the same things, don't we?' The answer is that 'it depends what material we're talking about'. What the canons don't allow is the use of a text from another Anglican Church in place of an authorized Church of England text. This, I know, has been a cause of frustration for some. An illustration of this in recent years concerned the provision of eucharistic prayers for children by the Church in Wales at a time when the Church of England was not seeking to produce its own. The General Synod has now asked that this provision should be made[15] and it is hoped that eucharistic prayers for use when significant numbers of children are present will soon be part of the Church of England's authorized liturgy. The Welsh prayers are not – and never have been – authorized for use in England.

However, texts from other Anglican churches may be used at those points in a service where an authorized text is not required. For instance, a form of intercession from *A Prayer Book for Australia* or a Prayer at the Preparation of the Table from the Canadian *Book of Alternative Services* may be included in a Church of England service. (The places where authorized texts are required are discussed fully in Chapter 4.)

There are some areas where the flexibility allowed is not immediately apparent. One such area is that of extended eucharistic prefaces. The notes on 'Planning and Preparing Holy Communion', in *New Patterns for Worship*, allow us to compose our own extended Prefaces for use with Eucharistic Prayers A, B and E. Guidance on how to do this is provided in *New Patterns* on pages 22–3 and on the related web site,[16] and there is fuller discussion of this in Chapter 4 (page 45). An extended preface from another Anglican church may, of course, be used in this context, and slotted between the dialogue and Sanctus in any of those three eucharistic prayers, provided it is in accordance with the doctrine of the Church of England.

So what about using worship resources from non-Anglican churches? The same applies here as to texts from other Anglican sources. Liturgical material from other churches cannot be used in place of an authorized text. A creed or authorized affirmation of faith, for instance, is a statement of faith which the General Synod has authorized on the basis that it expresses the Christian faith as the Church of England has received it. A credal statement from another church or tradition, while it might not contradict the doctrine of the Church of England, is nevertheless not an agreed expression of that doctrine.

The same goes for eucharistic prayers. The Church of England currently has twelve authorized eucharistic prayers in *Common Worship* (Prayers A to H in Holy Communion Order One, Prayers A and C in traditional language, and the Prayers in Order Two, traditional and contemporary; at the time of writing, two further prayers – for occasions on which significant numbers of children are present – are in preparation), in addition to the Prayer of Consecration in the BCP. Again, these have been carefully drafted, refined, revised and authorized so as to be faithful to the breadth of the Church of England's eucharistic theology and practice. A eucharistic prayer from another church or tradition does not necessarily express that same eucharistic theology and is therefore not authorized for use.

However, at those places where an authorized text is not required (see Chapter 4), material from other traditions may be used. Examples might include the use of a Blessing of Light from the Iona Community as part of the Gathering at an evening service, prayers from the Taizé Community for the intercession at Holy Communion, or texts for the dedication of church furnishings from the Church of Scotland's *Book of Common Order* (1994). In all such cases it is the minister's responsibility to ensure that the material used does not conflict with the doctrine of the Church of England.

Local Ecumenical Partnerships

Some different arrangements apply within Local Ecumenical Partnerships. This is governed by the ecumenical canons, Canons B 43 and B 44, and guidance on this is given in the Ecumenical Relations Code of Practice 1989.[17]

Fresh Expressions: A challenge to the status quo?

The developments around fresh expressions of church in recent years have raised serious questions for some ministers about the existing legal requirements for Anglican worship. Some have said that they find them too restrictive – a hindrance to mission, even. In some quarters, notions exist that fresh expressions stand outside the normal canonical framework. However, the fact remains that all licensed ministers make the Declaration of Assent on taking up their appointments and, as such, are bound to use in public worship only those forms or worship which are 'authorized or allowed by Canon'.

There is a sense, of course, in which official provision for worship in the Church of England has always played 'liturgical catch-up'. As far back as the eighteenth century, the first Methodists saw the need to develop a 'preaching service' which had greater freedom than was afforded by the non-eucharistic worship of the BCP. In the nineteenth century, Anglo-Catholic priests in the East End of London held 'mission services' in addition to formal celebrations of the Eucharist. In the late nineteenth century, the first cathedral 'nave services' were held – non-eucharistic acts of worship with a distinctly evangelistic focus – becoming a weekly fixture at St Paul's Cathedral in 1873. In 1967, the Church Pastoral Aid Society issued an order for 'Family Worship'. And yet it took until 1993 for the Church of England to give official authorization to a form for A Service of the Word (see Chapter 5 below) – a structure which would have provided for all these situations!

It is too early to say whether the flourishing of fresh expressions of church will in turn affect the official liturgical provision of the Church. Speaking in 2005 at the Liturgical Commission's residential conference, the Revd Dr Steven Croft, then Archbishops' Missioner and Team Leader of Fresh Expressions, observed:

> In terms of our liturgical development over the last fifty years we have witnessed a shift from unity established through common liturgical texts to unity established through common liturgical *shapes* . . . We are now, I sense, in the midst of a further shift from common shape to common *values* in our worship (and by extension) in our common life. It is, I believe, in the articulation and shaping of common Anglican **values** that we will find, preserve and deepen our unity as the Church of England.

This is a significant area for debate and one in which the Liturgical Commission and Fresh Expressions are currently engaged.

'The Ordering of Worship in Fresh Expressions of Church under Bishops' Mission Orders: Code of Practice for the Dioceses, Pastoral and Mission Measure 2007'[18] includes guidance on applying the canons to worship in fresh expressions. Some of the case studies in Chapters 5 and 6 are taken from fresh expressions of church.

Creativity *versus* policing?

All this talk of Canon Law, and what is, and is not, allowed in worship, can sound dry and dusty and more than a bit limiting – perhaps somewhat closer to St Paul's call for everything to be done 'decently and in order' (1 Corinthians 14.40) than his exhortation to live in the 'freedom of the Spirit' (cf. 2 Corinthians 3.17). It might seem at times that those who bear responsibility for ordering the Church of England's worship at a national level are acting as 'liturgical police'. St Paul, however, evidently did not think that there was inconsistency between the need for order and freedom. After all, the Spirit who brings freedom is the same Spirit who confers order. *Common Worship* bears this out in that it holds in a healthy tension both frameworks and freedoms. Two essential points, however, need to be made.

1. Because of our belief that it is primarily in worship that we express who we are as Anglican Christians, our core structures and core texts should express our understanding of the faith.
2. The purpose of the law concerning worship is to balance this need for order with a freedom to allow ministers discretion. As well as being faithful to our Anglican identity, we are also commanded to 'proclaim afresh [the faith of Christ] . . . in each generation'.[19] The freedom which the canons allow is designed to help us engage through worship with the communities in which we find ourselves, and to be effective in mission.

The canons are perhaps best seen as permission-giving, but with an underlying concern to maintain unity throughout the Church of England and a coherent expression of Anglican doctrine. Far from being a legislative straitjacket imposed from outside, they are products of the Church's common mind and, over time, may be changed as the whole Church sees fit. *Common Worship* – working within the canons – tries to enable flexibility within frameworks, to help local churches hold worship which is appropriate to their context, while remaining rooted in the essentials of the faith as the Church of England understands it. How that flexibility works is discussed in the following chapters.

3

Flexibility within the frameworks

A lot of the flexibility in *Common Worship* isn't always evident at first glance. We often have to scratch beneath the surface to find the 'soft' points among the 'hard' ones within the liturgy. In this chapter, we shall begin by looking at what we might call the 'fixed' services in *Common Worship* – those services published as a full liturgical text – looking particularly at

- Holy Communion Order One, and
- the Marriage Service,

and ask 'where is the freedom here?' The key often lies with the rubrics, so we go on to look at some of those to be found within *Common Worship*, what they mean and how they are to be read.

We then take a look at those parts of the *Common Worship* library which are not collections of services, but collections of resources, arranged in what is sometimes called 'directory' format. Finally, we shall unpack some of the other volumes which, though not advertised as resource directories, may also be used in this way. As we examine the broad selection of material provided for our use, we shall explore ways in which it may be used to season and enrich our worshipping diet.

Fixed services and flexibility

In Chapter 1, we saw something of the shift brought about by the introduction of CW – that it marked a new era for the worship of the Church of England in which structure has become the unifying factor across services, styles and worshipping traditions. Chapter 4 will look at those services in CW which have been authorized simply as structures. Some of the volumes of CW, and *New Patterns for Worship*, have been conceived as 'directories' of resources, to enable local creativity to flourish. But the fact remains that, throughout CW, there are still quite a number of fully worked-out services. At first sight, these might seem to be quite inflexible.

Take, for instance, the Eucharist of All Saints in CWT&S (page 548). This is a service with fully printed out texts for the Confession, Intercession and Dismissal. Where is the flexibility here, we might ask? But it's important to realize that, as with many of the services in CW for which a full text is provided, this is offered as an example of how something *might* be done, not of how it *must* be done. As it stands, this service would work very well indeed in a large building, such as a cathedral, with a large congregation and significant resources. A small church, though, wishing to celebrate Holy Communion on All Saints' Day (or All Saints' Sunday), would not necessarily be making the best choice in taking this model and transferring it wholesale to its local context. There is room for adaptation and, indeed, there is an *expectation* that those who plan worship locally will adapt and make best possible use of the flexibility allowed within the frameworks.

Even within the apparently 'fixed' services, there is considerable scope for flexibility, with 'soft' elements in and among the 'harder' fixed points. The following example shows this with reference to Holy Communion Order One.

Holy Communion Order One

The basic structure of this service (summarized on page 166 of CWMV) follows the typical fourfold pattern which underlies the whole of CW:

- Gathering
- Word
- Response
- Sending.

	The people and the priest
The Gathering	¶ greet each other in the Lord's name
	¶ confess their sins and are assured of God's forgiveness
	¶ keep silence and pray a collect
The Liturgy of the Word	¶ proclaim and respond to the word of God
	¶ pray for the Church and the world
The Liturgy of the Sacrament	¶ exchange the Peace
	¶ prepare the table
	¶ pray the Eucharistic Prayer
	¶ break the bread
	¶ receive communion
The Dismissal	¶ depart with God's blessing

Within this structure there are several non-negotiable (or 'hard') elements. Those marked* must use an authorized text:

- a liturgical greeting
- confession* and absolution*
- a collect*
- readings from Scripture including a Gospel reading
- a sermon (on Sundays and Principal Holy Days)
- the Nicene Creed (on Sundays and Principal Holy Days) or, on occasion, the Apostles' Creed or an affirmation of faith*
- intercessory prayer
- the Peace
- the preparation of the table
- a eucharistic prayer*
- the Lord's Prayer*
- the breaking of bread
- the distribution of communion
- a blessing
- a dismissal

Where an item does not need to follow an authorized text, the minister is free to select resources from within the provision for that service (e.g. the seasonal provisions for Holy Communion, CWMV, page 300), or from elsewhere (e.g. resources in NPFW, CWT&S), or in some cases to compose his / her own text.

In addition to the 'hard' elements of the service, there is considerable scope for 'soft' elements to be added. These include among others:

- hymns, songs, chants or other musical items provided by a choir worship group or instrumentalists
- recorded sound, video clips
- drama, interviews, discussion
- movement within the building
- ceremonial or symbolic action.

The expectation of *Common Worship* is that local churches will decide what is appropriate for their own context, and make decisions about elements which can be slotted into the given framework. Some examples of this are given in the case studies in Chapters 5, 6 and 7.

The Marriage Service

The Marriage Service is one where the non-negotiable elements are there for reasons that are legal as well as liturgical. The service is cast in two clear parts, but even here, the underlying shape of CW may be seen.

¶	Introduction	[The Preparation]
	The Welcome	
	Preface	
	The Declarations	
	The Collect	
	. . . .	
	Reading	[The Liturgy of the Word]
	Sermon	

¶	The Marriage	[The Liturgy of Marriage]
	The Vows	
	The Giving of Rings	
	The Proclamation	
	The Blessing of the Marriage	
	Registration of the Marriage	
	. . . .	
	Prayers	[The Prayers]
		. . . .
	[The Dismissal]	The Dismissal

Mission and customization

The Church of England's Weddings Project[20] has conducted extensive research among couples and clergy to find out what leads people to choose a church wedding. The research has revealed that couples who marry in church are more likely to 'stick' with church if the priest taking the wedding has taken the trouble to tailor the service for that couple. While there are some important non-negotiable elements in the marriage service, there are opportunities for customization. Priests are sometimes bombarded with requests: 'May we write our own vows?' 'Uncle Bill would like to read a lesson', 'What about lighting candles?' 'How about this poem?' Most of us want to meet couples where they are and be as accommodating as possible, but we need to understand where we have flexibility and where there are constraints.

Marriage liturgy isn't a free-for-all. The marriage service is an authorized text governed by law. When we sign registers, we confirm that we have married a couple 'according to the rites and ceremonies of the Church of England.' It's important that the service has been conducted according to an authorized rite – if not, questions could be raised as to the legality of the marriage. In seeking to be married in church, a couple is seeking to be married *by* the church, therefore within the living tradition of the church's liturgy. While some elements may be customized, others – particularly those with legal or doctrinal significance (e.g. the declarations and the vows) – are not open to change. There's a need, then, to balance the legally required elements of the marriage service with a genuine pastoral and evangelistic concern to meet the couple half-way and accommodate some of their thoughts and ideas about customization.

What's non-negotiable?

The following elements / sections of the marriage service must be included and in some cases (where stated below) the authorized wording has to be used (page numbers refer to CWPS):

- the **Preface** (p. 105) – either this version of that on p. 136 must be used;
- the **Declarations** (p. 106) – the authorized wording must be used;
- the **Collect** (p. 107) must be included;
- there must always be at least one **Reading from the Bible** (but see below);
- a **Sermon** is required;
  - but the minister has complete freedom as to its style and content!
  - the **Vows** (p. 108) – the authorized wording must be used;
- the **Giving of Rings** (p. 109) – the authorized wording must be used;
- the **Proclamation** (p. 110) – the authorized wording must be used;
- the **Blessing of the Marriage** (p. 111) – the wording on p. 111 or that on pp. 152–5 is used;
- the **Lord's Prayer** (p. 113) must be included;
- the **Dismissal** (p. 114).

Where's the scope for customization?

- The **Welcome** (p. 104):
  - *Common Worship Pastoral Service* offers suggested words for this, but there is freedom to use other appropriate words at the minister's discretion.
- The **Reading (s):**
  - For the biblical reading (s) there is enormous scope for choice;
  - CW suggests a range of biblical readings on pages 137–49 but others may be selected;
  - in addition to biblical readings, at the discretion of the minister, a non-biblical reading might be included;
  - sometimes a couple will suggest a reading. It's important that any non-biblical reading doesn't contradict or undermine the Christian view of marriage as the Church of England understands it. Discussion with the couple on the choice of a non-biblical reading is essential.

- The **Prayers** (page 112):
  - o the forms of prayer given on pages 112–13 and 156–68 are suggestions. Other prayers, possibly newly-written, might be used. In some contexts, it might be appropriate for extempore prayer to be offered during the Service.
  - o One very positive approach is to work together with the couple on choosing and / or writing prayers for their wedding. The prayers can be tailored to their own situation / needs and the exercise can be a very fruitful in terms of exploring the Christian faith.
  - o If someone else (e.g. a friend or family member) has offered to write prayers, it's important to give them clear guidance on length, style and content, and also to make sure that the prayers are seen well in advance of the service.
- **Hymns and songs** may be freely chosen,[21] as may any music played or sung before, during and after the service.
  - o *Common Worship* suggests where hymns might be sung (after the Welcome, before the Vows, at the Registration, after the Prayers) but they may be sung elsewhere (e.g. between two readings).
  - o The words and music (mp3 files) of a selection of popular wedding hymns are available at: www.yourchurchwedding.org/hymns-media-player.aspx
  - o It's vital that, in making musical choices, the particular resources of the local church are borne in mind. Widor's *Toccata* does not work well on a harmonium with C and F missing!
  - o Some couples might suggest including a secular song (sung or a recording played) within the service. Clearly, there should be careful consideration of the lyrics, their appropriateness to an act of Christian worship and of how they fit within the service as a whole.
- **Ceremonial:** the marriage service gives clear directions about essential ceremonial (e.g. the taking of hands at the Vows, and the joining of hands at the Blessing), but there are other places where additional ceremonial touches may be included.
  - o One popular custom in some churches is the lighting of a single large candle ('wedding candle') from two smaller candles, symbolizing the union of bride and groom.
  - o If either the bride or the groom is from another culture, it might be appropriate to incorporate a ceremonial custom from that culture within the service. If so, care needs to be taken that it does not interrupt the flow through the 'core' elements of the Vows, Giving of the Rings and Blessing.

Paul Bayes, the Church of England's Mission and Evangelism Adviser, has written about this from his standpoint both as a parish priest and as a leader of the Church of England's Weddings Project in Chapter 7 on page 143.

Holy Communion Order One and the Marriage Service are both 'fixed' orders in that they are published as complete texts in *Common Worship*. Yet within that text, there is scope for local variation, adaptation to a particular context and a degree of customization. So how do we spot the clues? What are the signs that one part of a service is flexible, while another is not negotiable? The clue very often lies in the rubrics.

How rubrics work

Common Worship is designed to be permission-giving: enabling churches to take local decisions about the specific style and content of worship, while remaining rooted in structures and key texts which are common to the whole Church. In order to make the most of the flexibility which is offered, we need to read carefully the rubrics – the instructions – which are printed throughout the text. They are easily visible, being printed (as is traditional) in red, and are the biggest clue to the amount of flexibility allowed. While some of the rubrics in CW are directive:

An authorized Eucharistic Prayer is used   (CWMV, p. 176)

others are intentionally permissive:

A minister uses a seasonal invitation to confession or these or other suitable words   (CWMV, p. 168)

The concept of 'other suitable words' was one which made an appearance in the ASB, and thus opened the way to previously unknown opportunities of freedom for ministers and worship leaders. In a sense, permissive rubrics are a natural outworking of the freedom given to the minister under Canon B 5 to 'make and use variations which are not of substantial importance' to authorized forms of service (see page 13). The rubrics throughout CW give clear directions and use particular wording to indicate the degree of freedom allowed:

- '*is used*' or '*is said*' indicates that something is non-negotiable;
- '*is normally used*' indicates that, although there is an expectation that something in the service will be present, there might be certain circumstances when a minister chooses to omit it;
- '*may be used*' means that the words in question may indeed be used, but that the minister is free either not to use them, or to do something else.

A word which crops up from time to time is 'suitable'. Here, the rubric is encouraging the minister to exercise the freedom he / she is allowed. As to what is 'suitable', that is up to the minister to decide, having regard to Canon B 5.

Sometimes, a rubric will include a mixture of directive and permissive instructions. A classic illustration of this occurs at the Peace in Holy Communion Order One, where we read:

The president may introduce the Peace with a suitable sentence, and then says

The peace of the Lord be always with you

In other words, the president may choose to use a (scriptural) sentence to introduce the Peace or may decide to have no introduction. Equally, he / she may decide to introduce it with some other words, scripted or extempore. If it is decided to use a sentence, the president will need to decide what in his / her view is a 'suitable' sentence. *Common Worship* offers a range of these in its Seasonal Provisions (CWMV, page 300, CWT&S and CWF), but the president is free to select from elsewhere at will. Having introduced (or not) the Peace, the president *must* then say to the congregation:

The peace of the Lord be always with you

These words are a non-negotiable element of that particular service.

When planning worship, it's always worth spending time looking at the rubrics. Very often they will show up a flexibility we didn't know was there. It might sound a bit strange, but while rubrics are not the heart of *Common Worship*, they are certainly a vital organ!

'Fixed-text' services don't in fact make up the greater part of *Common Worship*. Much of what we now have is offered to us not as 'services' but as 'resources' from which we are encouraged to build engaging and transformative worship.

Using directory resources

A key to the successful creative use of *Common Worship* is to get to know and understand those volumes which are collections or 'directories' of resources. The purpose of these books is to provide a wide range of material to help ministers plan worship appropriate to the local context within the authorized structures of *Common Worship*. In using them, it's vital that we have a clear knowledge of the structures involved and the 'hard' and 'soft' elements within them. We shall begin by looking at the three most significant 'directories':

- *New Patterns for Worship*
- *Times and Seasons* and
- *Festivals*

and then move on to look at two of the other *Common Worship* volumes:

- *Daily Prayer* and
- *Christian Initiation.*

We shall explore how they may be used as 'quarries' or 'resource banks' from which exciting material may be drawn. This means we sometimes need to think outside the box. Gone are the days of turning up to 'read the service'. I have a personal memory that illustrates the transition.

> When I was training for ordained ministry at Cranmer Hall, Durham, it was my privilege to be taught by the late Michael Vasey. Michael not only taught liturgy, he also used the college chapel as his laboratory – a place to road-test the latest offerings from the Liturgical Commission! The early 1990s was an exciting time in the liturgical life of the Church: seasonal worship was taking centre stage and the old patterns of Eucharist and Daily Prayer were being infused with new texts and actions. Half way through my training, we embarked on a wholesale revision of Daily Prayer: the old patterns of the ASB gave way to new forms. We began our new-style Daily Prayer at Advent. No longer did the service begin with the time-honoured words of the ASB, but with the liturgical action of lighting a candle and a 'blessing of the light'. One service in particular from that first week will always stick in my mind. It was led by a second-year ordinand who arrived rather late, hurrying and breathless. As he reached the leader's stall on the dot of 6.30, he picked up the service book, only to be confronted by a new and unfamiliar liturgy. Instead of greeting us with 'The light and peace of Jesus Christ be with you all', he blurted out, 'Um . . . I'll just light this candle.'

The publication of *Patterns for Worship* in 1995 was a landmark in Church of England liturgical publishing. This book – and its successor in the *Common Worship* era, *New Patterns for Worship* (2002), was conceived as a 'directory' of liturgical texts together with some selected examples to show how the material might be used in different contexts. This directory approach had begun to creep in a few years beforehand. *The Promise of His Glory* (1991), the seasonal resource book for the period of time from All Saints' Day to Candlemas, had included within each section several pages of 'Sentences and Prayers' for each season alongside the full orders of service for particular occasions. Two years later, *Enriching the Christian Year* – an unofficial publication, but compiled by members of the Liturgical Commission – was cast exclusively in directory format. The contents and layout of these books had a profound influence on the directory material in *Common Worship.*

New Patterns for Worship

NPFW is the Church of England's directory *par excellence*. Although it contains some sample services (pages 317–478) it's not really a book of services, but a book of resources – a book of ingredients. If we served someone a helping of flour, some yeast, water, fat and salt, instead of a piece of bread, they would have good reason to complain. NPFW is the flour, yeast, water, fat and salt. It's up to us, as leaders and planners of worship, to turn those ingredients into worship that will feed and sustain those who take part in it. NPFW divides into three sections.

1. Planning worship (pages 5–54)

- This section contains a great deal of excellent guidance on a host of issues around the planning and preparation of worship, including:
  o a Service of the Word
  o Holy Communion
  o music in worship
  o children in worship
  o space and colour
  o Common Prayer and the Law.

2. Resource sections (pages 55–316)

- This is the heart of the book and is a collection of texts for worship organized under headings which relate to structure:
  o Gathering and Greeting
  o Penitence
  o Liturgy of the Word
  o Psalms and Canticles
  o Creeds and Authorized Affirmations of Faith
  o Prayers
  o Praise and Thanksgiving
  o The Peace
  o Action and Movement
  o Conclusion.
- In some cases, the texts are also available in other *Common Worship* volumes. In others, they are to be found only in NPFW.
- As a further aid to planning, the texts are given a thematic tag, e.g. 'Holy Spirit', 'God in Creation', 'Mission' or 'General'. This is especially helpful when assembling themed worship.
- Included within the 'Liturgy of the Word' section is a helpful summary of the rules surrounding the use of an authorized lectionary in Church of England worship.

NPFW explains that 'the use of one of the authorized lectionaries' (from *Common Worship* or *The Book of Common Prayer*) around the main festivals serves to foster the sense that different worshipping communities are all 'telling the same story' (page 103). For this reason, there are periods of time during which an authorized lectionary should be used. The period is slightly longer for Services of Holy Communion than for non-eucharistic services:

- o For services of Holy Communion, an authorized lectionary should be used:
    - − From Advent Sunday until The Presentation (Candlemas);
    - − From Ash Wednesday until Trinity Sunday;
    - − On All Saints' Day.
- o For services of the Word, an authorized lectionary should be used:
    - − From the Third Sunday of Advent until the Baptism of Christ (First Sunday of Epiphany);
    - − From Palm Sunday until Trinity Sunday.

3. Sample services (pages 317–479)

- • This section offers 22 worked examples of eucharistic and non-eucharistic services for wide variety of occasions.

All the material in NPFW is also available to download, free of charge, from the Church of England's web site.[22]

Times and Seasons

Common Worship: Times and Seasons offers a rich feast of resources for the two great seasonal cycles within the Christian Year:

- • the Christmas (or Incarnation) Cycle – running from Advent Sunday to the Feast of the Presentation of Christ (or Candlemas) on 2 February;
- • the Easter (or Paschal) Cycle – running from Ash Wednesday to Pentecost.

There is also material for:

- • the period of time between All Saints' Day and Advent;
- • Trinity Sunday, Corpus Christi, Dedication Festival and Bible Sunday;
- • the Agricultural Year;
- • Embertide.

Within each section for each season, the book provides:

- • an introduction to the season;
- • seasonal worship material;
- • some 'fully worked' examples of services for major occasions (e.g. Ash Wednesday, All Saints' Day).

The introduction to the season gives some useful history and a 'theological map' of each period of seasonal time. It's often the case that our worshippers know little about the seasons of the Christian Year and their meaning – largely because no one has told them (!) – but would love to know more. What is offered here is a useful starter for teaching, preaching, or perhaps for including in seasonal service booklets.

The seasonal worship material follows the same basic pattern for each season. There are:

- invitations to confession
- *Kyrie* confessions
- Gospel acclamations
- intercessions
- introductions to the Peace
- Prayers at the Preparation of the Table
- extended prefaces
- blessings and endings
- (for some seasons) an alternative dismissal
- short passages of Scripture

These texts may be used to enrich a 'fixed' service (e.g. slotted into the appropriate places in Holy Communion Order One), but may also be used as ingredients for creating worship using one of the authorized structures (see Chapter 4).

There is also material here that can offer a helpful 'way in' to preaching through the seasons. The extended prefaces have been written in such a way as to encapsulate much of the essential theology of each season. The extended preface for the period from Epiphany to the Eve of Candlemas, for instance, refers to the three major emphases of the season:

- The visit of the wise men to the infant Jesus
- The baptism of Jesus by John in the River Jordan
- Jesus' first 'sign' at the wedding in Cana.

All honour and praise be yours always and everywhere,
mighty creator, ever-living God,
through Jesus Christ your only Son our Lord:
for at this time we celebrate your glory
made present in our midst.
In the *coming of the Magi*
the King of all the world was revealed to the nations.
In the *waters of baptism*
Jesus was revealed as the Christ,
the Saviour sent to redeem us.

In the *water made wine*
the new creation was revealed at the wedding feast.
Poverty was turned to riches, sorrow into joy.
Therefore with all the angels of heaven
we lift our voices to proclaim the glory of your name
and sing our joyful hymn of praise:

CWT&S, p. 133

The repetition of this preface on each of the Sundays of the Epiphany season might helpfully underpin a short seasonal sermon series drawing out the themes of the season:

'Who is Jesus?' – Sermon series for the Epiphany Season (Year C)

Day	Gospel reading	Sermon
Epiphany	Matthew 2.1–12	Jesus – King of all the world
Baptism of Christ (First Sunday of Epiphany)	Luke 3.15–17, 21–22	Jesus – Son of God and Saviour
Second Sunday of Epiphany	John 2.1–11	Jesus – bringer of new life

A word needs to be said about two groups of material which occur in each of the seasonal sections. The first of these is the 'Short passages of scripture'. Many people will remember – some with affection – the 'sentences' which were so much part of the culture of the ASB. (Introductory and Post Communion sentences were provided for use during the Order for Holy Communion Rite A.) CW has done away with the provision of 'official' sentences for Holy Communion but Note 4 (CWMV, page 330) reads:

Sentences of Scripture appropriate to the season and the place in the service may be used as part of the president's greeting, in the Invitation to Confession, at the Peace, before the gifts of the people are collected and after the distribution of communion.

Sentences can come into their own at midweek eucharistic worship. Without a hymn to set the tone at the opening, a sentence might helpful do a similar job, e.g. in Lent:

For thus said the Lord God, the Holy One of Israel:
In returning and rest you shall be saved;
in quietness and in trust shall be your strength.

Isaiah 30.15, CWT&S, p. 220

31

The Lord be with you
and also with you.

There are also other occasions (often at Services of the Word, or occasional services) where appropriate short sentences or passages of Scripture might usefully be employed. An example of this might be at Evening Prayer, to introduce the confession, e.g. in Advent:

The night is far spent, the day is at hand:
let us therefore cast off the works of darkness
and let us put on the armour of light.

Romans 13.12

The 'alternative dismissals' are a distinctive feature of *Times and Seasons* and help reinforce the link that exists between worship and mission. They are a creative reworking of a time-honoured practice within the Catholic tradition that, at the end of every Eucharist, 'the last Gospel', John 1.1–14, is read, as a reminder that the congregation (having been made one with Christ in the sacrament) is then to carry the gospel of the incarnate Christ into the world. In *Times and Seasons* there is a broader range of Dismissal Gospel passages, but with the same intention: they make the point that the dismissal is not simply about getting the ministers out of the way after Communion so that we can have coffee, but about sending us out to live the Gospel as transformed people.

The alternative dismissal usually takes this form:

- a hymn or song and /or an acclamation
- the reading of the Dismissal Gospel
- an extended (usually Trinitarian) blessing with congregational 'Amens'
- a seasonal dismissal versicle and response.

The following example is for the Advent season:

After the post communion prayers a hymn may be sung and / or the following acclamation may be used:

Acclamation

With love and compassion
come, Lord Jesus!

With judgement and mercy
come, Lord Jesus!

In power and glory
come, Lord Jesus!

In wisdom and truth
come, Lord Jesus!

The Dismissal Gospel

Hear the Gospel of our Lord Jesus Christ according to Mark
Glory to you, O Lord.

Jesus came to Galilee, proclaiming the good news of God, and saying, 'The time is fulfilled, and the kingdom of God has come near; repent, and believe in the good news.'

Mark 1.14–15

This is the Gospel of the Lord.
Praise to you, O Christ.

Blessing

May God the Father, judge all-merciful,
make us worthy of a place in his kingdom.
Amen.
May God the Son, coming among us in power,
reveal in our midst the promise of his glory.
Amen.
May God the Holy Spirit make us steadfast in faith,
joyful in hope and constant in love.
Amen.
And the blessing of God almighty,
the Father, the Son, and the Holy Spirit,
be among you and remain with you always.
Amen.

Dismissal

As we await our coming Saviour, go in the peace of Christ.
Thanks be to God.

CWT&S, p. 42

These alternative dismissals lend themselves to the use of symbol and creative movement within the church building. With a large congregation, it can be difficult for everyone to move, but it is usually possible for the minister(s) to move to another part of the church (perhaps to the font at Eastertide, or to the crib at Christmas / Epiphany) and for the congregation to turn and face in that direction. If the congregation is smaller, it is more likely that everyone will be able to gather – having perhaps moved during a hymn or song – and share in the dismissal together in a new location. An alternative dismissal may be incorporated within a service of Holy Communion or A Service of the Word. One word of warning, though – don't be afraid, if you are expanding this part of the service, to cut something inessential elsewhere in the service.

Times and Seasons also includes some additional resources which stand outside the normal pattern outlined above. The following four examples are particularly noteworthy.

1. Prayer for Personal Renewal – from the Pentecost section (page 493)

This is printed as part of a fully worked out Liturgy of the Feast of Pentecost, yet it is transferable to other occasions when the focus of the worship is the renewal of the Holy Spirit. Songs of invocation of the Spirit and of praise may be added, and when used in this way, this resource may be used as part of the gathering at a service of prayer and praise.

Prayer for personal renewal

Prayer for personal renewal and anointing may be offered here. Oil of chrism may be used. Alternatively, oil blessed specially for the occasion may be used.

Oil may be brought forward, the bearer saying
Oil for the renewal of God's people

The President says
Be with us Spirit of God;
Nothing can separate us from your love.

Breathe on us, breath of God;
Fill us with your saving power.

Speak in us wisdom of God;
Bring strength, healing, and peace.

If oil is to be blessed specially for the occasion the president says the following prayer.

Blessed are you, Sovereign God and eternal Father.
Daily your Spirit renews the face of the earth
bringing strength out of weakness,
hope out of despair and life out of death.
By the power of your Spirit
may your blessing rest upon those
anointed with this oil in your name.

Let it be for them
a sign of your acceptance and adoption,
your equipping and empowering;
Form in them the likeness of Christ
that they may be witnesses of your astonishing love,
and fill them afresh with life in all its fullness.
Blessed be God Father, Son, and Holy Spirit.
Blessed be God for ever.

Those who wish to receive this ministry of prayer may come forward.
Appropriate hymns and songs may be used.

When the prayer is ended the President says

Let us bless the Father, and the Son, and the Holy Spirit
Let us praise and bless God for ever!

CWT&S, p. 493

2. Thanksgiving for the Resurrection – from the Easter Liturgy section (page 421)

This may be used in a number of different ways through the Easter season. The whole text may be used at the beginning of the Eucharist throughout the season, following on from the opening greeting and being followed by the Gloria. It may also be used as a Processional at Evening Prayer. Section 2 of the text may be used alone in procession to or from the baptismal font.

3. Thanksgiving for the Holy Ones of God – from the section for All Saints to Advent (page 558)

This text may be used on various occasions, e.g. at Morning or Evening Prayer or other services at All Saints' tide. It may also be used at services of Christian initiation in procession to or from the font.

4. The Rogationtide Procession – from the Agricultural Year section (page 614)

This litany, together with some suggested readings, is offered as part of the resource for Rogationtide, as prayer for God's blessing on the crops. The compilers assume flexibility in how it is used: inside a building, outside, in a walk around a parish. It could also be very successfully developed into a 'prayer walk' around a local community, and the wording adapted or expanded to reflect the local context, whether that be urban or rural.

A resource which has made creative use of *Times and Seasons* is *Together for a Season: Seasonal Resources for All-age Worship*.[23] This series of three books expands and interprets the *Times and Seasons* material for a context in which all ages worship together, and in which visual and kinaesthetic elements play a crucial part alongside the text. Volume 1 covers the period from Advent to Candlemas, Volume 2 from Ash Wednesday to Pentecost, and Volume 3 focuses on creation, ordinary time and the period between All Saints' Day and Advent.

Festivals

Festivals was the last CW volume to be published (February 2008) and is a different sort of book from *Times and Seasons*. Whereas *Times and Seasons* is really a book for planning, *Festivals* is a book for use in church, principally by the president at Holy Communion. Nevertheless, it does include a large raft of worship material, arranged in 'directory' format, for the major Festivals and Feast Days of the year. For each Festival we are given all or some of the available:

- invitations to Confession
- *Kyrie* Confessions
- collects
- lectionary provision (Principal, 2nd and 3rd service)
- Gospel acclamations
- intercessions
- introductions to the Peace
- prayers at the preparation of the table
- short prefaces
- extended prefaces (for Prayers A, B, E)
- post communions
- blessings
- acclamations
- some short passages of Scripture

Once again, these are resources which can usefully be quarried and used either to enrich and develop 'stand-alone' services or to build services within outline structures.

Daily Prayer as a directory resource

Common Worship Daily Prayer is the most comprehensive daily prayer book the Church of England has ever known. Including forms for Morning, Evening and Night Prayer, Prayer During the Day and more informal patterns of prayer, it is an invaluable resource in helping sustain and develop a rich diet of daily prayer. It is also, though, a mine of resources which may easily be taken from this context and slotted into other services. There are several sets of material in particular which are well worth exploring:

The Acclamation of Christ at the Dawning of the Day (page 108)

This acclamation includes, after an opening versicle and response, the opening of Psalm 95 (*Venite*) and a 'Berakah' prayer:

Blessed are you, Sovereign God, creator of all,
to you be glory and praise for ever.
You founded the earth in the beginning
and the heavens are the work of your hands.
In the fullness of time you made us in your image,
and in these last days you have spoken to us
in your Son Jesus Christ, the Word made flesh.
As we rejoice in the gift of your presence among us
let the light of your love always shine in our hearts,
your Spirit ever renew our lives
and your praises ever be on our lips.
Blessed be God, Father, Son and Holy Spirit.
Blessed be God for ever.

The note to this states that the Acclamation of Christ at the Dawning of the Day may replace the Preparation as the start of Morning Prayer on any occasion. Similarly, it could be incorporated into a special service, or if the structure of A Service of the Word with a Celebration of Holy Communion is being followed (see Chapter 4), it could form the opening section of such a service.

Forms of Penitence (page 91)

Daily Prayer provides four Forms of Penitence. In addition to taking the place of the Confession and Absolution within a service of Morning or Evening Prayer, these could – on occasion – be used as a part of the penitential section within a service of Holy Communion. An example of this is given in the case studies in Chapter 6.

Prayers at the Foot of the Cross (page 317)

These prayers are designed for use on Fridays or other appropriate occasions (e.g. during Lent and Passiontide or on Holy Cross Day, 14 September). They could take the place of standard prayers of intercession at Holy Communion or a Service of the Word. The introductory rubric suggests that

A procession may be made towards a suitable cross, before which lights may be burning, or a cross may be carried in. It may be mounted upright or laid on the ground, with lights burning around it.

At the centre of the prayers stands (during silence or the singing of songs or chants) stands a powerful symbolic action:

. . . any of those present may come forwards to touch the cross. They may, for example, place their forehead on it as a sign of entrusting to God, in union with Christ and his suffering, their own burdens as well as those of others.

Thanksgivings

Daily Prayer provides forms of thanksgiving for

- the Word
- Holy Baptism
- the Healing Ministry of the Church
- the Mission of the Church

all of which have potential for use beyond the pages of the book. The Thanksgiving for the Word is included within the case study on page 97.

Psalm Prayers

For each of the psalms (and sections of the longer psalms), *Daily Prayer* provides a Psalm Prayer – a prayer which may be said instead of the *Gloria* and which both sums up some of the themes in the psalm but within a Christian frame of reference. Many of these prayers are very fine compositions and can easily be taken from here and used elsewhere, e.g. the prayer which follows Psalm 69:

Thirsting on the cross,
your Son shared the reproach of the oppressed
and carried the sins of all;
in him, O God, may the despairing find you,
the afflicted gain life
and the whole creation know its true king,
Jesus Christ our Lord.
Amen.

CWDP, p. 748

This prayer fits extremely well with the Gospel readings for the Feast of Christ the King in Years B (John 18.33–37) and C (Luke 23.33–43) and might therefore be a suitable prayer with which to conclude prayers of intercession on that day.

   Common Worship: Daily Prayer, then, as well as being a treasure trove of material for personal and corporate prayer each day, can also serve as a rich vein from which to quarry texts for slotting into established worship structures. Another book which can be used in the same way is *Common Worship: Christian Initiation.*

Resources in *Christian Initiation*

The definitive edition of *Common Worship: Christian Initiation* was published in 2006 and is a much more comprehensive resource than the interim edition (1998) which it replaced. It includes, on either side of the initiation services, two important sections of material:

- Rites on the Way: Approaching Baptism
- Rites of Affirmation: Appropriating Baptism.

And then, in the final section of the book come

- Rites of Reconciliation and Restoration: Recovering Baptism.

Although the Baptism and Confirmation services are 'fixed models', almost all the other material is conceived as resources from which selections may be made as needed.

Rites on the Way

The core of this section is the set of 'Rites Supporting Disciples on the Way of Christ'. Designed for use with enquirers and those on a journey towards baptism, these texts are an invaluable worship resource to balance the teaching input of courses such as *Alpha, Emmaus* and *Christianity Explored.* As with the whole of *Common Worship,* there is an expectation that ministers will draw on these resources both wholesale and piecemeal, making selective use for a variety of contexts and occasions.

From the 'Welcome of Those Preparing for the Baptism of Children' (p. 31), the Prayer for commissioning godparents or sponsors is one which may be used in church or as part of a pastoral prayer during baptism preparation:

N and N, you have been asked to nurture *these children* as they grow in faith.

May God bring you joy as you hold *them* in his love,
and walk with *them* on the Way of Christ.
May you be a blessing to one another,
and may the blessing of God almighty,
the Father, the Son and the Holy Spirit,
be among you and remain with you always.
Amen.

The 'Affirmation of the Christian Way' (p. 36), while designed for specific use with those moving towards baptism, might be used on any occasion in worship when there is a special focus on following the Way of Christ:

As we follow the Way of Christ,
we affirm the presence of God among us,
Father, Son and Holy Spirit.

God calls us to share in worship.
Jesus said, where two or three are gathered in my name,
I am there among them.
Jesus, you are the Way: guide us on our journey.

God calls us to share in prayer.
Jesus said, remain in me, and I will remain in you.
Jesus, you are the Way: guide us on our journey.

God calls us to share the scriptures.
Jesus met his disciples on the road
and opened the scriptures to them.
Jesus, you are the Way: guide us on our journey.

God calls us to share in communion.
Jesus said, do this in remembrance of me.
Jesus, you are the Way: guide us on our journey.

God calls us to share in service.
Jesus said, as you do it for the least of these, you do it for me.
Jesus, you are the Way: guide us on our journey.

God calls us to share the good news.
Jesus said, go and make disciples of all nations.
Jesus, you are the Way: guide us on our journey.

A rite from this collection which has many possibilities is that of the Presentation of the Four Texts. These are core Christian texts:

- The Summary of the Law
- The Lord's Prayer
- The Apostles' Creed
- The Beatitudes.

They may be given to 'disciples on the way' on a succession of occasions throughout their preparation for baptism or confirmation. The texts are available to buy as a set of 'Words for Life' cards from Church House Publishing.[24] For each of the texts, *Christian Initiation* provides a rich raft of supporting material:

- some supporting lections
- words of introduction
- the text itself
- a concluding prayer.

The Summary of the Law (page 41), for example, provides as follows.

One of the following or other readings may be used

Exodus 20.1-19; Leviticus 19.9-18; Romans 8.1-4; Romans 13.8-10; Galatians 5.13-14; Mark 12.28-34

One of the following psalms may be used

Psalm 1; 15; 119.9-16; 119.97-104

The minister addresses those who are disciples on the Way of faith.
Brothers and sisters, listen carefully to the words that Jesus gave us as a summary of the law. These few words help us understand how we are to live as human beings in God's world. They are given not to condemn us but to show how by the grace of God we may live as free people reflecting the goodness and love of God.

The Summary of the Law is read:

Our Lord Jesus Christ said:
The first commandment is this:
'Hear, O Israel, the Lord our God is the only Lord.
You shall love the Lord your God with all your heart,
with all your soul, with all your mind,
and with all your strength.'

The second is this: 'Love your neighbour as yourself.'
There is no other commandment greater than these.
On these two commandments hang all the law and
the prophets.

The minister says

God of truth,
help us to keep your law of love
and to walk in ways of wisdom,
that we may find true life
in Jesus Christ your Son.
Amen.

In addition to the intended context, these texts could be used in a variety of other situations:

- the readings could provide lections for a service focusing on the law and Jesus' summary of it
  - in regular Sunday worship as part of a teaching series in the 'open' lectionary season
  - as part of a devotional or teaching programme during Lent
  - or for a service of readings, music and reflection, following a sequence such as the following.

Exodus 20.1-19
Psalm 1
Leviticus 19.9-18
Psalm 15
Romans 8.1-4
Psalm 119.9-16
Romans 13.8-10
Psalm 119.97-104
Galatians 5.13-14
Canticle: *A Song of God's Love* (1 John 4.7-11,12b)
Mark 12.28-34
The Summary of the Law

- The concluding prayer is a useful prayer, in the style of a collect, which might on occasion be used to conclude prayers of intercession, as a post communion, or as a prayer to follow a time of silence after a reading on the theme of law.

Rites of Affirmation

In the same way, texts from the Rites of Affirmation may be quarried for use elsewhere. The Thanksgiving for Holy Baptism (page 184) is designed for use several weeks after a baptism has taken place, and includes the words of the Commission (page 185). Experience has shown that this text – which forms an optional part of the baptism service – is often omitted for reasons of time. It is, though, an excellent text and may be used, not only several weeks after a person's baptism, but on any occasion when there is a commissioning for a particular ministry or office.

The minister would first introduce the ministry for which the person is to be commissioned, then lead the Commission:

Those who are baptized are called to worship and serve God.
Will you continue in the apostles' teaching and fellowship,
in the breaking of bread, and in the prayers?
With the help of God, I will.

Will you persevere in resisting evil,
and, whenever you fall into sin, repent and return to the Lord?
With the help of God, I will.

Will you proclaim by word and example
the good news of God in Christ?
With the help of God, I will.

Will you seek and serve Christ in all people,
loving your neighbour as yourself?
With the help of God, I will.

Will you acknowledge Christ's authority over human society,
by prayer for the world and its leaders,
by defending the weak, and by seeking peace and justice?
With the help of God, I will.

Eternal God, our beginning and our end,
preserve in your people the new life of baptism;
as Christ receives us on earth,
so may he guide us through the trials of this world
and enfold us in the joy of heaven,
where you live and reign,
one God for ever and ever.
Amen.

CWCI, p. 185

The minister may then add a prayer of commissioning and a blessing.

The Affirmation of Baptismal Faith (page 197) is designed for those who are already baptized and confirmed, but who wish, after preparation and instruction (e.g. having followed a nurture course) to make a public act of personal Christian commitment. There is a often a strong pastoral need for a resource which enables those who were baptized as infants but have come to a living personal faith later in life to make such a declaration, without denying the fact of their baptism. This rite meets that need and, significantly, it uses water. However, it is very definitely not rebaptism! The rubric at the 'water' part of the service is worded very carefully:

The candidates may come forwards to the font and sign themselves with water, or the president may sprinkle them.

In churches where the baptismal font is a pool designed for immersion baptisms, there is nothing to prevent the person entering the water – though, significantly, no words are used, and they perform the action themselves. A case study showing the use of this rite is given in Chapter 7 on page 136.

Reconciliation and Restoration

The final section of *Common Worship: Christian Initiation* is Reconciliation and Restoration: Restoring Baptism (page 227). It contains the first official reconciliation rites the Church of England has ever had, with the exception of the specific case of the provision in the BCP Visitation of the Sick. The Commentary by the Liturgical Commission notes that

The resources and forms of service for Reconciliation and Restoration are intended to meet some of the situations in which the Church confronts the fact of human weakness and sin and appropriates again the new life proclaimed in baptism.

CWCI, p. 353

As well as two forms for the Reconciliation of a Penitent, this section includes a rich bank of penitential resources under the umbrella of A Corporate Service of Penitence (page 239):

- sentences
- opening prayer
- resources for prayer and penitence
- invitations to confession
- *Kyrie* confessions
- a table of readings
- Gospel acclamations
- a form of intercession
- the Lord's Prayer
- introductions to the Peace
- Prayer at the Preparation of the Table
- short prefaces
- extended preface
- acclamation
- blessings
- ending

These are an invaluable addition to the seasonal and thematic items included in *Times and Seasons* and *New Patterns* and may be used to expand an existing penitential section of a service, or in the crafting of seasonal worship during Lent.

Common Worship is full of resources which, if used wisely and well, can enrich our worship and help make it a place of encounter with God and potential transformation. But if we are to make the best use of these resources, we need to know what is available. There is no substitute for spending time trawling through one volume after another and asking: 'Where might I use that prayer?' It is not an easy task to change the culture from being a church of one or two service books, to a church which encourages (and expects) diversity and variety in worship. A thorough knowledge of the directory resources in *Common Worship* and *New Patterns* will help.

But these resources only fully come into their own when we use them with the most radical part of *Common Worship* – the authorized structures.

4

Authorized structures

Common Worship is much more than a successor to what went before it. The authorized services include far greater opportunities for local freedom than have previously been known in the Church of England. Yet its most radical contribution lies not in its texts but in its structures. Not only does a common structural framework underpin everything within its covers, but its most flexible contents are services which consist only of an authorized structure and no text.

The groundbreaking Report *Faith in the City* (1985), which examined the life of the Church in an urban context, included among its recommendations a clear directive to the Liturgical Commission (through the General Synod) to 'pay close attention to the liturgical needs of churches in urban priority areas'.[25] *Faith in the City* set down on paper what had been known for some time: that the word-laden services of the ASB were failing to connect with congregations and that, as a result, they were hindering the Church in its mission. The result of this recommendation was a move towards an official recognition of the need for diverse patterns of worship, and the eventual authorization of A Service of the Word in 1993. This structure was followed by the first 'directory-style' liturgical book, *Patterns for Worship*, in 1995. For the first time, it was officially possible to express certain freedoms in worship while remaining genuinely Anglican – in other words, not throwing out the baby with the bath water!

As we saw in Chapter 1, one of the basic principles at work in *Common Worship* is that it is uses a common structure as a means of articulating 'common prayer' across the Church of England, rather than everyone praying the same words at the same time. In all *Common Worship* volumes and across the full range of services, the 'family likeness' of the fourfold structure is visible:

Gathering – Word – Response – Sending.

But the presence within *Common Worship* of services that have been authorized purely as liturgical structures reveals this fourfold shape even more clearly. The three structures are:

1. A Service of the Word

This can be found in CWMV, pages 21–7, and online.[26]

2. A Service of the Word with a Celebration of Holy Communion

This can be found in CWMV, page 25, and online.[27]

3. An Outline Order for Funerals

This is in CWPS, page 257, and online.[28]

Structures are not, of themselves, exciting; it's what we do with them that matters. Here, more than anywhere else in *Common Worship*, the minister and the local church are being asked to show vision and creativity, as dry bones are given sinews, flesh and spirit and come alive.

For each of the three structures, we shall look at

- how the structure is put together, and the elements within it;
- how we can draw on resources throughout *Common Worship* to bring the structures to life.

A Service of the Word

The Introduction to A Service of the Word (ASOTW) on page 21 of CWMV reads: 'A Service of the Word is unusual for an authorized Church of England service. It consists almost entirely of notes and directions and allows for considerable local variation and choice within a common structure.'

ASOTW provides a structure which enables a local church to put together an act of non-eucharistic worship in a form which suits the local context, while retaining essential elements and a clear sense of Anglican identity. Examples of services of the word might include:

- Morning, Evening or Night Prayer
- all-age worship
- a service of prayer and praise
- an act of collective worship in school
- a service to mark a special occasion (e.g. civic service)
- a contemplative service
- an act of 'alternative worship'.

In fact, there is really no end to the possibilities which exist within this structure. In Chapter 5, we hear from churches which have used ASOTW to create a wide variety of types of worship across a range of contexts and traditions, from a service for World Human Rights Day to Liquid Worship for Mothering Sunday, and worship for an after-school club.

As with all *Common Worship* services, ASOTW is cast in four clear sections:

> ¶ **Preparation**
> ¶ **The Liturgy of the Word**
> ¶ **Prayers**
> ¶ **Conclusion**

I now outline in more detail each of these four sections and the elements which they contain.

Preparation

This opening section includes the following elements.

> • A **Greeting**, by which the minister welcomes the people
> • **Authorized Prayers of Penitence**
> • **Praise**
> • The **Collect**

In other words, what happens here, at the start of the service, is that the worshippers are gathered and formed into a worshipping community. As one of the greetings from *New Patterns* reminds us:

> We come from scattered lives to meet with God.
> Let us recognize his presence with us.
>
> *Silence is kept.*
>
> As God's people we have gathered:
> **let us worship him together.**

The minister – presiding over the congregation – welcomes the people in God's name and leads them in penitence, in praise and in prayer.

Within the Preparation, a great deal of flexibility is possible. The following section describes some of the possibilities.

Prayers of Penitence

The Prayers of Penitence may be omitted from the Preparation and included later as part of the Prayers section. What is important is that, when they do occur, an authorized form is used.

- **Authorized Confessions** may be found in the following places:
  - in CWMV, pp. 122–32, 276–8
  - in NPFW, pp. 81–90

o   in CWPE, pp. 509–18
o   in CWPS, p. 261.

- *Kyrie* **Confessions:** a note on page 133 of CWMV reads: 'Short sentences may be inserted between the petitions of the *Kyrie*, suitable for particular seasons or themes. The insertion of such sentences may replace any form of confession, provided that the sentences are of a penitential character and are followed by an authorized form of absolution.' These '*Kyrie* Confessions' offer opportunities for local creativity. CW offers many 'worked examples' of these, for instance:
  o   in CWMV, pp. 133–4, 277–8
  o   in NPFW, pp. 91–4
  o   in CWPE, pp. 505–6, 519–20
  o   in CWPS, p. 118
  o   in CWT&S, as part of the provision for each season
  o   Prayers of Penitence for use at the Advent Wreath in CWT&S, pp. 56–7
  o   in CWF, as part of the provision for each occasion
  o   in the Reconciliation and Restoration section of CWCI, p. 255.

In each case, these are *models* to show how *Kyrie* Confessions might be constructed, rather than a fixed list of texts.

- **Introducing the Confession:** the minister may invite the congregation to confess their sins with any suitable words. Examples of this may be found throughout CW:
  o   in the Seasonal Provisions of CWMV, pp. 300–29 and at www.cofe.anglican.org/worship/liturgy/commonworship/texts/hc/seasonal/seasonalfront.html
  o   in NPFW, pp. 77–80
  o   in the CWPE, p. 503
  o   in CWT&S, as part of the provision for each season.

Once again, these are models which may be used as they stand, or as the basis for newly composed invitations to confession. In some traditions, it is the norm for a confession to be introduced *extempore*, or with a series of scriptural verses following the singing of songs.

- **Authorized absolutions** may be found here:
  o   in the *Common Worship CWMV*, pp. 135–7, 279
  o   in *New Patterns for Worship*, pp. 95–7
  o   in the *President's Book*, pp. 507, 521–3
  o   in the Reconciliation and Restoration section of *Christian Initiation*, pp. 288–9.

Peter Craig-Wild once wrote that 'Anglican worship tends to assume that the human body consists of two buttocks and two ears.'[29] One of the exciting developments in worship during the past 20 years is the discovery (or rediscovery) of a multi-sensory dimension in worship. The prayers of penitence are a classic case of a part of the liturgy which is open to considerable creativity and the inclusion of multi-sensory elements. Books such as Sue Wallace's *Multi-sensory . . .* series[30] and *Together for a Season*[31] offer a range of engaging possibilities. The following example, adapted from Peter's *All-age Service for Ash Wednesday* gives one illustration of how this might be done. This is a multi-sensory interpretation of The Liturgy of Penitence for Ash Wednesday from *Common Worship: Times and Seasons.*[32]

The minister introduces the Prayers of Penitence

As we gather as God's people, let us now call to mind our sin and the infinite mercy of God.

God the Father,
have mercy on us.

God the Son,
have mercy on us.

God the Holy Spirit,
have mercy on us.

Trinity of love,
have mercy on us.

Silence is kept for reflection.

Most merciful God, Father of our Lord Jesus Christ, we confess that we have sinned in thought, word and deed.

The congregation is then encouraged to move around a number of 'Sorry Stations' positioned around the building:

- *a 'Repentance Rope' – a large plain rope and a pile of small pieces of red wool*
  - *people can to tie a piece of wool to the rope to represent their sin*
- *a 'Sand Spread' – a large box or sandpit filled with sand*
  - *the congregation is encouraged to make a hand print on the sand to represent their sin*
- *some 'Sin Stones' – some large pebbles and a large bowl*
  - *people take a stone, feel its weight and in their imagination use it to represent their sin, before placing it in the bowl*
- *paper, pencils, a bin and an office shredder*
  - *people write or draw on a piece of paper something for which they want to ask forgiveness, and place it in the bin*

The use of the 'Sorry Stations' may be accompanied by silence or by quiet music.

As the movement around the stations comes to an end the minister encourages the congregation to finish the prayer of confession:

We have not loved you with our whole heart.
We have not loved our neighbours as ourselves.
In your mercy
forgive what we have been,
help us to amend what we are,
and direct what we shall be;
that we may do justly,
love mercy,
and walk humbly with you, our God. Amen.

The Absolution is spoken:

The Lord enrich *you* with his grace,
and nourish *you* with his blessing;
the Lord defend *you* in trouble and keep *you* from all evil;
the Lord accept *your* prayers,
and absolve *you* from *your* offences,
for the sake of Jesus Christ, our Saviour.
Amen.

A person at each of the Sorry Stations then performs one of the following actions:

- *The Repentance Rope is hung on a large wooden cross;*
- *The Sand Spread is raked level;*
- *Water is poured over the Sin Stones;*
- *The paper in the bin is shredded.*

I have used this rite[33] in many different contexts, but have always found that it makes a profound impression on the worshippers – perhaps the most marked was that of hearing the grinding sound of an office shredder after the Absolution during a service for a group of Archdeacons!

Praise

Within the Preparation, a variety of forms of praise is envisaged. In some contexts, this might include formal versicles and responses, or the singing of a canticle (e.g. *Venite*), while in others, this might take the form of singing a hymn or a set of worship songs. Where musical items (traditional or contemporary) are being chosen for this opening time of praise, it is important to ask whether, as well as helping the congregation to praise, they also help the congregation to gather. The hymn *Forth in thy name, O Lord, I go* and the song *Thuma mina (Send me, Lord)* are both excellent within their own traditions, but definitely not for gathering!

Two publications which give helpful advice on the selection and positioning of hymns and songs in worship are *Sing God's Glory*[34] and the RSCM's quarterly liturgy planner *Sunday by Sunday*.[35] For churches which use the CW Second Service Lectionary, helpful suggestions are given in *Sunday by Sunday for the Second Service Lectionary*.[36]

The Collect

A collect should be used to round off this preparatory section, or it may come later in the service, to conclude the prayers. There is a real danger that the collect can be seen as 'one of those Anglican things which must be done' rather than an element in the liturgy which genuinely enables the prayer of God's people. Problems happen when the purpose and nature of the collect is misunderstood.

The point of a collect is that it 'collects' together the prayers of the people. If used at this point in a service, the collect sums up the gathering of God's people: their praise and penitence.

Praying a collect
The act of praying a collect has three parts:

1.   An introductory bidding by the minister

The simplest form of this might be 'Let us pray'. Alternatively, a longer, more focused bidding may be given, such as that for Ash Wednesday in CWT&S:

Let us pray for grace to keep Lent faithfully.

CWT&S, p. 224

The bidding does *not* run: 'The Collect for the Twelfth Sunday after Trinity'!

2.   Space for prayer

It is vital that space is given for the congregation to pray in stillness.

3.   The text of the Collect, said by the minister, to which the congregation replies 'Amen'.

The congregational parts of a Collect are the silent prayer and the final 'Amen'. Collects are not designed to be prayed aloud by the whole congregation.

One of the most effective uses of a collect is as the conclusion of a time of sung praise. Following an extended set of worship songs, instrumental music may continue and there could be a time of 'singing in the Spirit'. The collect provides an excellent conclusion to this, spoken as a 'voice-over' by the minister. (See the case study on page 110.)

Where collects can be found
- CW provides two sets of collects for the Christian Year. The first set, published in 1997 and included within CWMV in contemporary language on pages 375–447, and in traditional language on pages 448–520, owes much to the traditional Cranmerian models in the BCP, most of which are themselves based on prayers of the ancient Church. The second, a set of additional collects, was published in 2004. These prayers, though rich in imagery, are shorter and more direct in style. They are published as part of the most recent editions of CWCPC and are also available online.[37]
- Most of the CW Collects are all printed with a longer, Trinitarian ending, as in the following example:

Almighty God,
whose Son Jesus Christ fasted forty days in the wilderness,
and was tempted as we are, yet without sin:
give us grace to discipline ourselves in obedience to your Spirit;
and, as you know our weakness,
so may we know your power to save;
through Jesus Christ your Son our Lord,
who is alive and reigns with you,
in the unity of the Holy Spirit,
one God, now and for ever.

While this longer ending is 'to be preferred at Holy Communion',[38] the minister may shorten the ending to

through Jesus Christ our Lord.

To which the congregation responds 'Amen'.
- Whereas in the ASB, the collects for each Sunday were thematically linked to the Sunday theme and readings, that is not the case in CW. Here, in Seasonal Time, the collect will tend to focus on some aspect of the season but in Ordinary Time, the collects are of a more general nature and stand apart from the readings of each 'proper'.
- The set of additional collects includes one or more for each season which are marked with an asterisk. Each of these, it is suggested, would be suitable to be used as a collect throughout an entire season. This has obvious advantages in helping a congregation become familiar with a particular prayer over a number of weeks.

Eternal Lord,
our beginning and our end:
bring us with the whole creation
to your glory, hidden through past ages
and made known
in Jesus Christ our Lord.

CWCPC, p. 15

The Liturgy of the Word

The Liturgy of the Word includes the following elements.

¶   **Readings (or a reading) from Holy Scripture**
¶   A **psalm**, or, if occasion demands, a scriptural song
¶   A **sermon**
¶   An **authorized Creed**, or, if occasion demands
¶   An **authorized Affirmation of Faith.**

Readings

Anglicans have always taken Scripture seriously, and one of the dangers of some worship today is that, compared with that of previous generations, it can be rather light in the biblical department. On the other hand, it is possible to have too much of a good thing! One of the concerns of many who plan and lead worship is that, as Anglicans, we are sometimes in danger of drowning in a sea of words, and that we are failing to reach those whose learning (and worshipping) preferences are either visual or kinaesthetic.

What is crucial is that ASOTW includes a significant portion of Scripture. The authorized structure anticipates 'at least two readings from the Bible' but allows that there may be only one reading 'if occasion demands'. The introduction and notes to ASOTW[39] refer to 'different and adventurous ways' of presenting Scripture, and mention dramatic and responsive reading. Creativity is to be encouraged.

At certain times of the year, the readings should be taken from an authorized lectionary. This is so that 'the whole Church is together proclaiming the major events in the Christian story'.[40] The period when this applies is as follows:

- The Third Sunday of Advent to the Baptism of Christ;
- Palm Sunday to Trinity Sunday.

For the remainder of the year, it is 'open season', giving the opportunity for a thematic approach to the choice of readings or to the continuous reading of a book of the Bible from week to week, thus reflecting the time-honoured tradition in some churches of 'sermon series'.

Psalms

Specific reference is also made to a psalm. The demise of psalms in worship is one of the more unfortunate consequences of the move away from Matins and Evensong as the staple diet of Anglican parish worship. Often, because psalms had come to be associated with a particular way of singing them (namely Anglican chant), they have disappeared altogether. Valiant attempts to reintroduce them through metrical and song-style settings (e.g. *Psalm Praise*,[41] *Psalms for Today* and *Songs from the Psalms*[42]) were not entirely successful. It does seem, though that there has been a recent shift in attitude. Graham Kendrick, speaking at the 'Deep Calls to Deep' symposium at the London School of Theology in September 2008, spoke of the need to restore psalmody as a core feature of Christian worship. For a brief but comprehensive account of various ways of using psalms in worship, see Anne Harrison, *Recovering the Lord's Song: Getting Sung Scripture back into Worship.*[43]

ASOTW does, though, allow a 'scriptural song' as an alternative to a psalm. CW is simply packed with such songs, called canticles. The best source of these is CWDP, pages 547–646, and the online collection.[44]

These scriptural songs may be sung to help us reflect with one piece of Scripture on another. As the late Michael Vasey used to say, 'Liturgy is just a way of doing the Bible!' What we are still lacking, though, are musical settings of these words – in a broad range of styles.

Sermon

Although the term 'sermon' is used, Note 7 to ASOTW makes clear that 'the term "sermon" includes less formal exposition, the use of drama, interviews, discussion, audio-visuals and the insertion of hymns or other sections of the service between parts of the sermon'. A sermon is mandatory on Sundays and Principal Holy Days but not at other times.

Creed/Affirmation of Faith

The same applies to the creed, or an authorized affirmation of faith – which may be omitted, except at the principal service on Sundays and Principal Holy Days.[45] In addition to versions of the Nicene, Apostles' and Athanasian Creeds, CW provides 7 affirmations of faith. These are printed in the CWMV, pages 139–48, and in NPFW, pages 158–66. The third of the affirmations of faith is a metrical version, by Bishop Timothy Dudley-Smith, of the Apostles' Creed. Interestingly, this is only the second time in the history of the Church of England that a hymn has received authorized status. (The other is Bishop John Cosin's version of *Veni creator spiritus* in the 1662 Ordinal.) No other affirmations of faith or credal hymns have authorized status within the Church of England.

Prayers

The Prayers include the following elements:

> ¶ **Intercessions and thanksgivings**
> ¶ **The Lord's Prayer**

When God's people meet for worship, they give thanks and pray for others. Both these elements should be present within the prayers at ASOTW. Holy Communion Order One suggests that prayers usually include the following concerns and that they might follow this sequence:

- the Church of Christ
- creation, human society, the Sovereign and those in authority
- the local community
- those who suffer
- the communion of saints.

Other than that, there is complete freedom as to the words and actions we might use in prayer.

The Lord's Prayer is a mandatory part of all authorized services in the Church of England, and should be used in one of its three authorized forms:

- The contemporary version (CWMV, p. 178)
- The version in *The Book of Common Prayer* 1662 (also in CWMV, p. 64);
- The 'modified traditional' version (CWMV, p. 178).

Conclusion

> The service concludes with a **blessing, dismissal** or other **liturgical ending**.

The concluding part of ASOTW is designed to send out God's people in mission. There is an assumption that, in worship, we meet with God, are changed by the encounter and that this encounter will make a difference to the way we live in the world. There is always the danger of making the Conclusion too brief: the rite of transition from prayer to coffee, as it is in some churches! If we are serious about making links between worship and mission, then it can sometimes be helpful to make this explicit in the way we are sent out to do God's work in the world.

Common Worship: Times and Seasons includes a number of 'alternative dismissals' which seek to do just that. They work on the basis that we should go with the gospel ringing in our ears, and include a verse or two of Gospel which reminds us of our call to mission. The following example is from the Alternative Dismissal for the Easter Season:[46]

Acclamation

A hymn may be sung and/or the following acclamation may be used

Alleluia. Christ is risen.
He is risen indeed. Alleluia.
Praise the God and Father of our Lord Jesus Christ.
He has given us new life and hope.
He has raised Jesus from the dead.
God has claimed us as his own.
He has brought us out of darkness.
He has made us light to the world.
Alleluia. Christ is risen.
He is risen indeed. Alleluia.

The Dismissal Gospel

Hear the Gospel of our Lord Jesus Christ according to John.
Glory to you, O Lord.
Jesus said, 'I am the resurrection and the life. Those who believe in me, even though
they die, will live, and everyone who lives and believes in me will never die.'

John 11.25,26

This is the Gospel of the Lord.
Praise to you, O Christ.

The Blessing

God the Father,
by whose love Christ was raised from the dead,
open to you who believe the gates of everlasting life.
Amen.
God the Son,
who in bursting from the grave has won a glorious victory,
give you joy as you share the Easter faith.
Amen.
God the Holy Spirit,
who filled the disciples with the life of the risen Lord,
empower you and fill you with Christ's peace.
Amen.
And the blessing . . .

The Dismissal

With the power that raised Jesus from the dead at work within you, go in the
peace of Christ. Alleluia, alleluia.
Thanks be to God. Alleluia, alleluia.

A Service of the Word with a Celebration of Holy Communion

In this section, I shall be exploring the shape and content of the second authorized framework within *Common Worship*. If there were a prize for the most convoluted title for a church service, this one would surely win it for the Church of England! Hopefully those churches who make use of this excellent authorized structure will give their service a rather more user-friendly name.

What A Service of the Word with Holy Communion does is apply the priciples of A Service of the Word to eucharistic worship. Structurally, the outline is identical to that of ASOTW, with an additional section *The Liturgy of the Sacrament* between the Prayers and the Dismissal.

¶ Preparation
¶ The Liturgy of the Word
¶ Prayers
¶ The Liturgy of the Sacrament
¶ The Dismissal

The introductory note reminds us that it should not normally be used as the regular Sunday or weekday service. However, it could, for instance, be used on those occasions when a slightly more informal celebration of Holy Communion is held, e g. in churches which hold a monthly all-age celebration of Holy Communion.

As with ASOTW, there is considerable scope for freedom within the given framework. In the printed outline (CWMV, page 25), those sections which must follow an authorized text are helpfully marked with an asterisk. Most of the points which relate to ASOTW also therefore relate directly to this service as well.

Preparation

The people and the priest:

¶ greet each other in the Lord's name
¶ confess their sins and are assured of God's forgiveness*
¶ keep silence and pray a Collect*

The Preparation is identical to the corresponding section in ASOTW.

The Liturgy of the Word

The people and the priest:

¶ proclaim and respond to the word of God

As with ASOTW, the Liturgy of the Word should contain

- readings (or a reading)
- a sermon
- an authorized creed or an authorized affirmation of faith.

One of the readings, though, at a service of Holy Communion, must be a Gospel reading. This might be the only reading, or it might follow a reading from the Old or New Testament.

Prayers

The people and the priest:

¶ pray for the Church and the world

The Prayers section is the same as that in ASOTW except that in a Communion Service, the Lord's Prayer could come in its more usual place immediately after the eucharistic prayer, rather than being prayed as part of the prayers of intercession.

The Liturgy of the Sacrament

The people and the priest:

¶ exchange the Peace
¶ prepare the table
¶ pray the eucharistic prayer*
¶ break the bread
¶ receive Holy Communion

The contents of the Liturgy of the Sacrament are taken from Holy Communion Order One. In the paragraphs which follow, we shall look at the component parts of this section and how we might resource them.

The Peace

The basic form of this is given in Holy Communion Order One (CWMV, page 215). *Common Worship* provides a wide range of sentences with which to introduce the Peace. These may be found:

- in CWMV (p. 290 and pp. 300–29)
- in NPFW (pp. 272–7)
- as part of the seasonal material in CWT&S
- as part of each set of material in CWF.

Once again, these are suggested models, and ministers are free to introduce the Peace with sentences of their own choice or composition, perhaps to reflect the theme of a service or a particular emphasis of the sermon.

It is worth remembering that the Peace does not have to happen at this particular point in the service. It may be used:

- as the opening greeting (in the Preparation section);
- before the Breaking of the Bread (i.e. after the eucharistic prayer);
- at the Dismissal.

Some excellent practical advice on introducing, sharing (and ending!) the Peace is given in NPFW (pages 269–71).

Preparation of the Table

After the sharing of the Peace (if this is done in its 'normal' location), the table is prepared for Holy Communion.

Prayers may be used at the Preparation of the Table. CWMV provides twelve suggestions (pages 291–3), and further prayers may be found in CWT&S and CWF. Of course, there is nothing to stop a minister using an appropriate prayer from another source, or writing a suitable prayer of his or her own.

While the Prayer at the Preparation of the Table is normally a prayer spoken by the president at Holy Communion, Prayer 8 in the CWMV may be spoken by members of the congregation (children or adults):

With this bread that we bring
we shall remember Jesus.

With this wine that we bring
we shall remember Jesus.

Bread for his body,
wine for his blood,
gifts from God to his table we bring.
We shall remember Jesus.

The Eucharistic Prayer

An authorized eucharistic prayer must be used at A Service of the Word with a Celebration of Holy Communion. The reasons for this have been discussed in Chapter 2. But as has already been mentioned, there is flexibility for us to use locally-composed extended prefaces with Eucharistic Prayers A, B and E.

Extended Prefaces
CW provides extended prefaces for Ordinary Time and for Seasons in:

- CWMV (pp. 294, 300–29)
- in CWT&S
- in CWF.

These may be used as they stand, or taken as models upon which to base newly composed texts.

Another excellent source of material is the 'Praise and Thanksgiving' resource section in NPFW (pages 219–67). Many of these texts can be slotted into Eucharistic Prayers A, B or E between the opening dialogue and the Sanctus, e.g. the following Thanksgiving on the theme of Church and Mission:

> Sovereign Lord, creator of heaven and earth and sea,
> and everything in them,
> we are your people, we give you thanks.
> **We praise your holy name.**
>
> You shake us and fill us with your Spirit,
> you stretch out your hand to heal,
> to do signs and wonders through the name of Jesus.
> We are your people, we give you thanks.
> **We praise your holy name.**
>
> Jesus is the author of life,
> handed over to be killed for us.
> You raised him from the dead,
> and made us whole in him.
> We are your people, we give you thanks.
> **We praise your holy name.**
>
> Not many of us are wise by human standards,
> not many are influential,
> not many of noble birth.
> We are your people, we give you thanks.
> **We praise your holy name.**
>
> You choose the foolish to shame the wise,
> you choose the weak to shame the strong,
> the lowly and despised,

so no one may boast before you.
We are your people, we give you thanks.
We praise your holy name.

Your strength is made perfect in our weakness.
Your grace is enough for us.
We are your people, we give you thanks.
We praise your holy name.

cf Acts 4.24,30,31; 3.15,13; 1 Corinthians 1.26-29;
2 Corinthians 12.9

Therefore with angels and archangels . . .

In composing our own extended prefaces, care must be taken to match the style and length of the whole prayer. The following helpful guidance given in NPFW (page 222) should be followed:

If the Preface is specially composed, the president says, 'And now we give you thanks . . .' and then offers brief thanksgivings in the form 'We thank you that . . .' or similar words. They normally include thanksgiving for

- creation;
- redemption;
- the continuing work of the Spirit.

They should not conclude with 'Amen'. (This is reserved for the very end of the eucharistic prayer.) The president concludes by saying 'Therefore with angels and archangels . . .' (Prayers A, B and C) (or) 'And so we gladly thank you, with saints and angels . . .' (Prayer E).

It needs to be noted that Eucharistic Prayers D, G and H are structured differently and are therefore not suitable for use with extended prefaces.

Acclamations
Eucharistic Prayers A and F both have optional acclamations printed within the prayer:

To you be glory and praise for ever. [Prayer A]

Amen. Lord, we believe. / Amen. Come, Lord Jesus. /
Amen. Come, Holy Spirit. [Prayer F]

Note 18 to Holy Communion Order One (CWMV, page 333) mentions that 'other acclamations may be used', which allows freedom to interject suitable words of our own choosing (said or sung) into the text of the Prayer.

Sanctus, Benedictus and Doxology
The Sanctus ('Holy, holy, holy Lord . . .') occurs in all CW eucharistic prayers, and the Benedictus ('Blessed is he who comes . . .') may be included

in all except prayer H. While prayers B, C, E and F end with a 'Great Amen', prayers A, D and G end with a doxology ('Blessing and honour and glory and power . . .'). The Sanctus, Benedictus and Doxology may be:

- said (using the words printed in CW)
- sung, as part of a communion setting
- sung in metrical form
- replaced by a worship song or hymn which performs the same function (see, for example, the use of Nathan Fellingham's song *Holy is the Lord God almighty* in the case study on page 112).

Breaking of the Bread and Giving of Communion

Note 20 to Holy Communion Order One (CWMV, page 334) stipulates that the words provided must be used on Sundays and Principal Holy Days, but that on other days the bread may be broken in silence or during the Agnus Dei.

Order One provides two sets of words (CWMV, page 179), and others may be found in CWT&S:

- for the Christmas and Epiphany seasons (p. 167)
- for Easter (p. 369) and All Souls (p. 569)
- for Ascension Day (p. 479).

The Dismissal

> The people and the priest:
>
> ¶ depart with God's blessing.

The Dismissal is identical to the corresponding section in ASOTW. Again, the option of using one of the alternative dismissals from CWT&S should be considered as a means of emphasizing the link between worship and being sent for mission.

The Outline Order for Funerals

As a curate, I once visited a family following the death of a man in his 90s. I was met at the door of the house by the man's daughter. We talked on the doorstep for about 3 minutes and then she asked, very hesitantly, whether I would like to come in and have a cup of tea. I replied that I would, followed her into the house and was installed in the living room. 'I'm sorry if you thought I was odd,' said the woman, 'but the last time we had a funeral in the family was about 30 years ago, and then all the Rector did was stand on the doorstep, check my mum's name, confirm the time of the funeral and say "I'll see you at the crematorium, then!" '

The days of the 'off the peg' funeral, where the minister simply turns up and 'reads the service', are gone – and thank goodness for that! Many ordained or licensed ministers would agree that funerals are often one of the greatest joys of pastoral ministry, offering the chance to make real connections between human life and the Christian gospel. Around us, there is a growing awareness that funerals can be 'special' – bespoke. In some places, secular 'funeral celebrants' offer tailor-made ceremonies to those seeking a non-religious funeral, and in some cases these events are thoughtfully put together and genuinely honour the memory of the person who has died. There is no need for a Christian funeral to be any less so: a well-planned service can be a moving occasion which both does justice to the Christian gospel, and recognizes the specific qualities of the person who has died. A Christian funeral, of course, involves the crucial additional dimension of pastoral support and follow-up.

Common Worship provides a 'written-out' authorized Funeral Service (CWPS, pages 258–73). But it also offers us an authorized outline order for funerals (page 257). This provision reflects that fact that the Church recognizes

- that we minister in a rich diversity of pastoral situations;
- that a single order of service will not meet the needs of everyone;
- that there will be occasions when all ministers will need to construct something other than a 'non-standard' funeral service.

At the same time, it's clear that a free-for-all is not acceptable: certain elements must be present if the service is to be recognizable as an act of Christian worship from within the Church of England. The Outline Order for Funerals is an authorized framework not unlike that of A Service of the Word. The basic fourfold shape is there (Gathering – Word – Prayers – Dismissal) with the additional elements of Commendation and Committal.

Certain elements in the Outline Order are mandatory. These are highlighted in **bold**. But by far the majority are optional, and so may be omitted, included or developed in a way which is appropriate to the person.

The Gathering

1. The coffin may be received at the door by the minister.
2. Sentences of Scripture may be used.
3. **The minister welcomes the people and introduces the service.**
4. A tribute or tributes may be made.
5. Authorized Prayers of Penitence may be used.
6. The Collect may be said here or in the Prayers.

The only essential element of the Gathering is that there must be a welcome and introduction. In other words, the minister taking the service must gather those present as a worshipping congregation and set the context for what is to follow. In so doing, he/she might wish to make use of material from the CW Funeral Service. Equally, he/she might feel it appropriate to use his/her own words. Other than this welcome and introduction, other elements are optional:

- the coffin may be met at the door by the minister, or may already have been brought into the church or chapel;
- the minister might read from Scripture, or there might be silence, a hymn, or music to listen to;
- there is the opportunity, once the congregation has been gathered, for tribute(s) to the deceased person to be made;
- prayers of penitence may be used – if they are, they must use an authorized text (see page 47 above);
- the Gathering may end with the Collect, or this may be used later to gather together the prayers.

Readings and sermon

7. **One or more readings from the Bible is used.**
   Psalms or hymns may follow the readings.
8. **A sermon is preached.**

In the second part of the service, we must read at least one reading from the Bible and we must preach. Until the arrival of CW in 2000, sermons at funeral services were optional. Now they are mandatory. This enshrines an important point: that funerals are first and foremost about the Christian hope of resurrection. A funeral will of course include elements which relate to the deceased person – it recalls and celebrates their life, it involves their commendation to God and the committal of their body – but all this is done within the context of a service which proclaims what Christians believe about death and eternal life. The preaching of resurrection at funerals is part of the fabric; hence it is required.

Prayers

9. **The prayers** usually follow this sequence:
   ¶ Thanksgiving for the life of the departed
   ¶ Prayer for those who mourn
   ¶ Prayers of Penitence (if not already used)
   ¶ Prayer for readiness to live in the light of eternity

There must always be prayers at a funeral but in this Outline Order, discretion is given to the minister to decide what and whom to pray for, and in what way. A steer is given as to what 'usually' happens, but within this framework, freedom is considerable.

Commendation and farewell

> 10. **The dead person is commended to God with authorized words.**

The Commendation of a dead person to God is a crucial part of any Christian funeral service, and springs from our faith in the resurrection. Because of the importance of this, Commendation has to take place with authorized words – we are not allowed to write our own! CW provides (CWPS, pages 272–377) a total of 17 sets of authorized words from which the minister is free to make a choice.

The Committal

> 11. **The body is committed to its resting place with authorized words.**

Once again, at the Committal, we are required to use authorized words from the range offered in CW (CWPS, pages 268–9).

The Dismissal

> 12. The service may end with a blessing.

The outline order makes clear that the service must have a clear ending and suggests that it may end with a blessing. However, the minister is free to end the service as he or she thinks fit. CW offers a number of suitable 'endings', one of which may be used, the Grace may be said, or locally-composed words may be used.

A case study of a funeral assembled using this authorized Outline Order can be found on page 140.

These three authorized structures from *Common Worship* offer a real opportunity for local creativity which makes the link between the worshipping life of the church and its context. The flexibility within them means that we do not have to become enslaved to the same forms of service week in week out, nor do we have to drown in a sea of words! They are the most radical part of *Common Worship* though, rather ironically, they account for less than ten printed pages of the whole! But they do represent very clearly the s*pirit* of *Common Worship* and an understanding that freedom and flexibility are to be encouraged within a mixed-economy church as we proclaim afresh the faith of Christ to our generation.

It's one thing knowing the theory but another putting it into practice. It's one thing having the structures nicely sorted in our minds, but another making informed selections of material to infuse those structures with life. And it is often a considerable step from crafting liturgy on the computer (or page) to enabling God's people to meet him in vibrant, transformative worship.

In the chapters which follow are some case studies which give examples of how the authorized services and structures have been interpreted by a range of ministers in various worshipping contexts. They are not examples of how worship must be done, but of how it has been done, and might be done, and they are offered in hope that they will inspire us all to try our hand at creativity in our own situation.

5

Case studies: *A Service of the Word*

As we have seen, *A Service of the Word* provides an authorized framework which allows a great deal of flexibility. The case studies in this chapter show a variety of ways in which this framework has been used to put together services which meet differing worshipping needs and which span a range of traditions and situations. For each one, the 'dry bones' of the structure are taken as the starting point, resources are drawn from *Common Worship* and elsewhere to create an act of worship which is right for the given context. All these services show the *Common Worship* 'family likeness' and are therefore recognizably Anglican, but the differences between them show that ASOTW is anything but a liturgical straitjacket.

- **An all-age carol service**

Tim Lomax writes about how his church built a Christmas carol service which was accessible to all ages and visitors.

- **Prayer Book Evensong revisited**

Peter Moger shows how a 'set piece' Prayer Book service can be transformed with the use of seasonal material, movement and projected images.

- **A service for World Human Rights Day**

This is a 'special occasion' liturgy – put together by Ally Barrett and Peter Moger – to celebrate the 55th anniversary of the Universal Declaration of Human Rights.

- **All-age liquid worship for Mothering Sunday**

Tim Lomax applies the principles of liquid church to produce a flexible and mission-shaped act of worship.

- **After-school club worship: a midweek Fresh Expression**

Tim Stratford writes about a fresh expression of church in his parish: an after-school club whose worship is not only part of the weekly programme but also a crucial part of the parish's work of Christian formation.

An all-age carol service

Tim Lomax

The Revd Tim Lomax is Assistant Curate in the parish of Penn Fields, Wolverhampton, and a member of the Liturgical Commission. Before ordination he ministered as a musician and worship leader. In the following section he gives some context for this order of service.

Background and context

All-Age Sunday. When do you have yours? Fourth Sunday, Fifth Sunday, First and Third Sundays when it's a leap year – or only when there's an 'R' in the month? And how do people take to it? Is it the morning when most of the congregation has a long lie-in? The week when people complain that the services are light on teaching, or that the message is over the children's heads or patronizing to adults?

A friend once said to me that for all-age worship to work you have to be an all-age community. What she meant was this: for all-age worship to hit the mark and scratch the itch, those present have to be in community with each other – friends concerned for each other, wanting the best for each other, putting the needs of each other first. The young need to be connected to the older generations and vice versa. This approach then impacts upon the worship itself as the congregation is not simply a disconnected group of individuals looking for their needs to be met, but a family. The church where I minister is discovering the joys of being an all-age community. It has not been without its trials but we have seen the difference it has made, not least to the worship. There is a warmth, a friendliness and a sense of encouragement. All ages are keen to engage in worship together. Congregation members and lay leaders are also eager to get involved and creativity is thriving. Use of audio-visual material is one such example. Themes are explored through film clips and the leadership team is creating its own high-quality presentations. In order to comply with copyright a Christian Video Licence has been acquired.[47]

Building on these developments we decided to add a new service to our usual repertoire of Christmas acts of worship – an all-age carol service. This would bring together different sections of the community, including children and parents from the thriving toddler groups, and the children and parents of the large junior schools in the parish who would participate in the service. The planning team used the basic Service of the Word structure as a framework – and ideas from the commended outlines for Crib and Christingle Services (CWT&S, pages 92–3) – for a creative act of worship that aimed to engage all ages, connect with the lives of those present and welcome the many visitors. The prayers and many of the other ideas were inspired by the Advent and Christmas material in *Common Worship: Times and Seasons*.

When brainstorming ideas, the team was keen to attempt to start where people were at, and then through the service explore God's story and the difference that can make to us. Suggestions and ideas for practical ways of responding were also considered important. It was felt that it was not appropriate to include an affirmation of faith especially as there were so many visitors, including those of other faiths. One member of the PCC wondered about the legality of this, but then discovered that 'the law' didn't require it on this occasion!

It was decided to try and involve as many people as possible in the leading of worship (whether by lighting candles or playing in the music group) and to ensure that this spanned all age groups. The service itself seemed like an extension of the regular church all-age worship. The place was packed, the atmosphere was great and there was a buzz of expectation. From the reactions of children, teenagers and adults as they chatted over refreshments at the end, it was clear that the service had provided a welcome opportunity to enter much more deeply and spiritually into the Christmas celebrations.

The service

The service started with a 'collage' of Bible passages read out while different topical headlines were shown on the PowerPoint display.

All-age carol service

Theme: *Hope in the doom and gloom*

¶ Gathering

LIGHT v. DARKNESS

The lights are put out.
   Candles are lit during the reading of these Bible verses.

Bible verse 1
In the beginning the Word already existed, he was God, he created everything there is. Life itself was in him and this life gives light to everyone.

Headline 1
30,000 jobs at risk as two major chain stores go in to administration.

Bible verse 2
Jesus said 'I am the light of the world.'

Headline 2
Mother gives internet warning after daughter, 13, who felt fat and ugly, kills herself.

Bible verse 3
The one who is the true light, who gives light to everyone was going to come into the world.

Headline 3
50% increase in people struggling to pay their mortgages.

Bible verse 4
The light shines through the darkness and the darkness can never extinguish it.

SONG – *Light of the world (sung by candlelight)* (CMP 1086, SOF 1419, TS 1406)

Welcome and introduction *(supported by PowerPoint presentation)*

OPENING PRAYER

> Lord Jesus, light of the world,
> born in the city of Bethlehem,
> born to be King;
> be born in our hearts this Christmas,
> be King of our lives today.
> **Amen.**

Adapted from CWT&S, p. 51

¶ Word

PERFORMANCE SONG *(from the school choir)*

MONOLOGUE – 'Doom and gloom'

> How have you fared in 2008? We'll do well to leave it behind unscathed won't we? Unemployment rising, recession looming, violent crime increasing, job prospects decreasing, house prices crashing, the cost of living spiralling, stress levels soaring, divorce rate climbing, numbers of companies going under mounting.
>
> All this doom and gloom seems to pile up like heaps of rubbish, polluting the life we want to have, crowding out our dreams. Life seems to be littered with this mess. And all this big rubbish is piled on top of the everyday rubbish – the stresses and strains of life – struggling with work, struggling to make ends meet, struggling to find time for the kids, struggling to look after Mum or Dad, struggling with coursework, homework, SATS.
>
> As if things couldn't get much worse, now we have Christmas to contend with – overspending, overeating, over-enthusiastic about inviting Auntie Nancy to visit on Christmas Day. But Christmas

shouldn't add to the doom and gloom, should it? After all, we don't wish each other a miserable Christmas, we say 'Happy Christmas'.

If Christmas does what it says on the tin, it should bring with it a ray of hope, shine a bit of light in the darkness, give us a reason to be cheerful. But is that even possible in a world like this?

HYMN – *Once in royal David's city*

PERFORMANCE SONG *(from the school choir)*

CHRISTMAS POEM *(read by school children)*

PERFORMANCE SONG *(from the school choir)*

READING – Isaiah 11.1-5 *(read by school head teachers)*

TALK A *(supported by PowerPoint presentation)*

- Show still picture of Wall-E (Main character in Disney's *Wall-E*) in the midst of the rubbish, or
- ask for volunteer to put on the mask and do a Wall-E impression!
- What a load of rubbish! In fact in Wall-E's day, the whole earth is covered by rubbish, every inch of it. The human race left earth 700 years earlier because the planet could no longer sustain life.
- Wall-E is a remnant of an army of robots whose job is to sort and clear rubbish. He is a great character – dedicated, charming, good-natured (a lot like me really!) and for a robot incredibly caring.

FILM SCENE – *Wall-E's Treasures and Trinkets (from bonus features)*

TALK B

- In the movie, Wall-E is helping shift the rubbish in the wasteland that is planet earth.
- He makes a very unlikely saviour of the human race, but it is Wall-E who makes room for the green shoot of promise. It is he who clears away enough of the rubbish to discover that there are signs of life.

FILM SCENE – *A day at work: Discovering the green shoot of hope*

TALK C

- You know – the more I watch this film, the more I can't help but make the connection – **this is God's story**.
- Sending someone to live among the rubbish, bringing hope like a green shoot of promise in all the doom and gloom, bringing new life, a brighter future . . .

¶ Response

TAKE AWAY

- *During the following hymn, the congregation is given **a tea light and a postcard:** 'How to pray this Christmas'.*
- *The postcard gives guidance as to how to pray and words to use, church contact details and details of other Christmas services.*

HYMN – *O little town of Bethlehem*

INTERCESSORY PRAYER (Audio-visual)

- Who do you think needs some light in the darkness – some hope in the midst of doom and gloom?
- Pray quietly as the pictures and music prompt you.

HYMN – *O come, all ye faithful*

CONCLUDING PRAYER

> Lord Jesus, light of the world,
> you shine light in the darkness
> and save your people in trouble.
> give peace in our hearts this Christmas
> and show all the world God's love.
> **Amen.**

Adapted from CWT&S, p. 52

THE LORD'S PRAYER

¶ Sending

MOVIE – Pictures linked with the song *Don't let the bells end – The Darkness*

NOTICES

BLESSING

> Children of God be glad!
> Your God loves you,
> giving you hope in sadness
> and turning the darkness to light.
> Be strong in hope therefore,
> for your God has come to save you.
> and the blessing . . .

Adapted from CWT&S, p. 52

Prayer Book Evensong revisited

Peter Moger

Why, you might ask, does a book on using *Common Worship* include a case study on Book of Common Prayer Evensong? The reason lies in the mixed economy present within *Common Worship*: Evening Prayer from *The Book of Common Prayer* is included within the Main Volume of *Common Worship* (pages 72–9).

The service of Evening Prayer, which first appeared in the 1549 *Book of Common Prayer*, was formed from elements of the monastic services of Vespers and Compline. It is one of Cranmer's works of genius and a characteristically 'Anglican' contribution to the worship of the Church. In its 1662 form, it is still alive and well in the early twenty-first century, both in parish churches (where it is said or sung) and in cathedrals where, as Choral Evensong, it attracts large congregations and a weekly BBC radio broadcast.

It is a service of the word, in which Scripture has pride of place and in which, through the use of canticles, one passage of the Bible is allowed to shed light on another. At its best it is unhurried and reflective – an opportunity for worshippers to hear the words of Scripture and be fed by them. BCP Evensong is often regarded as a 'set piece' which must on no account be tinkered with. On the one hand, that is absolutely right – Cranmer's service makes sense as it is, and is a beautiful form of liturgy. But on the other, its presence within the mixed-economy *Common Worship* begs the question 'Are there ways in which it might helpfully be revisited?'

One of the areas in which the BCP might seem to be lacking, when compared with much of the worship of today, is that of seasonal emphasis. Even in its material for Holy Communion, the seasons are marked only by a small number of proper prefaces. Queen Victoria, on returning from church one Easter Day was once heard to say 'Such a sad service for such a happy day.' And she was right; there is very little of the resurrection in BCP Holy Communion (even on Easter Day). In Evensong, too, apart from the lectionary readings and the collect of the day, there is nothing which reflects the season. Traditionally, a seasonal emphasis has been created by the choice of appropriate hymns and (where there is a choir) choral music. What *Common Worship* offers is the chance to use additional material to give the service a seasonal flavour.

In many places, BCP Evensong is attended by worshippers for whom the Prayer Book is a core element of their spirituality. It has nurtured Anglicans for over 450 years and continues to do so. Because of this, it's vital to treat a BCP service with respect, but this does not mean that we can't add other elements to it.

It makes sense, then, to leave the core of BCP Evensong untouched, but additions before and after can enhance the service without destroying its essential character. To adapt BCP Evensong in this way falls clearly within the provisions of the authorized structure of A Service of the Word. By framing the BCP core with seasonal gathering and dismissal rites we can give the service a clear seasonal identity. These additions can also open up possibilities for multi-sensory elements and for movement within the church building.

The shorter form of Evening Prayer – beginning with the versicle 'O Lord, open thou our lips' – is prefaced in *Common Worship* by the full penitential introduction from the BCP. But there is nothing to stop us replacing this penitential opening with another gathering rite, before moving on to the core of the Prayer Book service. Also, as the 'Schedule of Permitted Variations' (CWMV, page 80), reminds us, 'other prayers of intercession and thanksgiving may be used' (note 7), 'hymns may be sung . . . silence may be kept after the readings, a sermon may be preached, and the service may end with a blessing' (note 8).

Context

At St Matthew's, there was a long-standing tradition of a weekly sung BCP Evensong in the chancel. It attracted a congregation of about 25, of whom about 12 sang as part of the choir. One Pentecost, the service was expanded to give it a seasonal flavour, marking the end of the 50 days of Eastertide. The conclusion of the service included the removal of the Easter Candle from the Sanctuary (where it had been since the Easter Vigil) to the Font, and the dismissal of the congregation at the church door. Seasonal material from *Common Worship: Times and Seasons* was chosen to flank BCP Evensong.

The service

Evensong for Pentecost

¶ Preparation

The service begins in the chancel

> The love of God has been shed abroad in our hearts through the Holy Spirit who was given to us.
>
> *Romans 5.5*

INTRODUCTION

> Jesus Christ, whom we worship, is our crucified, risen and ascended Lord
> and we have walked with him through his journey of love.
> We have faced the agony of his suffering and death on a
>   cross.

We have rejoiced at his bursting free from the bonds of death.
We have enjoyed his risen presence with us
and his revelation of himself through the breaking of bread.
We have seen his return to the throne before which every knee
    shall bow
and every tongue confess that this Jesus is Lord.
And now, with the followers of his own time,
we await the coming of the promised Holy Spirit, his gift to his
    people,
through whom we make Christ known to the world.

RESPONSORY

As we wait in silence,
fill us with your Spirit.

As we listen to your word,
fill us with your Spirit.

As we worship you in majesty,
fill us with your Spirit.

As we long for your refreshing,
fill us with your Spirit.

As we long for your renewing,
fill us with your Spirit.

As we long for your equipping,
fill us with your Spirit.

As we long for your empowering,
fill us with your Spirit.

Silence is kept.

CWT&S, pp. 491–2

¶ **Evening Prayer** from the BCP / CW (CWMV, pp. 75–9)

RESPONSES (O Lord, open thou our lips . . .)

HYMN: *Come, holy Ghost, our souls inspire*

PSALM 67*

OLD TESTAMENT READING: Joel 2.21-32*

After the reading, silence is kept and the following response is used:

Thy word, O Lord, is a lantern to our feet:
and a light upon our path.

CANTICLE: *Magnificat*

NEW TESTAMENT READING: Acts 2.14-21*

After the reading, silence is kept and the following response is used:

Thy word, O Lord, is a lantern to our feet:
and a light upon our path.

CANTICLE: *Nunc Dimittis*

THE APOSTLES' CREED

†PRAYERS (Lesser Litany, The Lord's Prayer, Versicles and Responses)

COLLECTS

ANTHEM: *Listen, sweet dove* (Words: George Herbert, Music: Grayston Ives)

ADDRESS

¶ **Dismissal**

BLESSING OF LIGHT

The minister moves to the Easter Candle.

Blessed are you, sovereign God, overflowing in love.
With Pentecost dawns the age of the Spirit.
Now the flame of heaven rests on every believer.
Strong and weak, women and men tell out your word;
the young receive visions, the old receive dreams.
With the new wine of the Spirit
they proclaim your reign of love.
Amid the birth pangs of the new creation
the way of light is made known.
Source of freedom, giver of life,
blessed are you, Father, Son and Holy Spirit.
Blessed be God for ever.

CWT&S, p. 501

Each member of the congregation has a candle which is lit during the following hymn.

HYMN: *Come down, O Love divine*

During the hymn, the Easter Candle is carried in procession to the place of baptism. The congregation follows.

COMMISSION

> For fifty days we have celebrated the victory of our Lord Jesus Christ over the powers of sin and death.
> We have proclaimed God's mighty acts and we have prayed that the power that was at work when God raised Jesus from the dead might be at work in us.
>
> As part of God's Church here in N, I call upon you to live out what you proclaim.
> Empowered by the Holy Spirit, will you dare to walk into God's future, trusting him to be your guide?
> **By the Spirit's power, we will.**
>
> Will you dare to embrace each other and grow together in love?
> **We will.**
>
> Will you dare to share your riches in common and minister to each other in need?
> **We will.**
>
> Will you dare to pray for each other until your hearts beat with the longings of God?
> **We will.**
>
> Will you dare to carry the light of Christ into the world's dark places?
> **We will.**
>
> *The Easter Candle is extinguished in silence.*

CWT&S, p. 501

CONCLUSION

> The Lord is here.
> **His Spirit is with us.**
>
> Today we have remembered the coming of God's power on the disciples and we invite that same Spirit to drive us out into the wild places of the world.

HYMN: *Lord of the church, we pray for our renewing*

During the hymn, the ministers and people process out of church, or to the church door.

May the Spirit,
who hovered over the waters when the world was created,
breathe into you the life he gives.
Amen.

May the Spirit,
who overshadowed the Virgin when the eternal Son came among us,
make you joyful in the service of the Lord.
Amen.

May the Spirit,
who set the Church on fire upon the Day of Pentecost,
bring the world alive with the love of the risen Christ.
Amen.

And the blessing of God almighty,
the Father, the Son, and the Holy Spirit,
be among you and remain with you always.
Amen.

Filled with the Spirit's power,
go in the light and peace of Christ. Alleluia, alleluia.
Thanks be to God. Alleluia, alleluia.

CWT&S, pp. 501–2

Notes to the service
    * from the Second Service Lectionary provision for the Day of Pentecost (Year A).
    † The Versicles and Responses (which owe their origin to intercessory prayers in pre-Reformation monastic offices) are accompanied by images and captions projected onto a screen as an aid to intercession.
    It is vital that a significant silence is kept between the projection of each image and the singing (or saying) of the versicle and response.
    The following sequence is followed:

1	Image: cross / crucifix	*The first image is projected.*
	Caption 'Let us pray . . .'	*Silence is kept.*
		O Lord, shew thy mercy upon us.
		And grant us thy salvation.
2	Image: the Queen / someone in authority	*The second image is projected.*
		Silence is kept.
	Caption '. . . for those in authority'	O Lord, save the Queen.
		And mercifully hear us when we call upon thee.

3   Image: the bishop / local church
     congregation
     Caption '. . . for the Church and its
     leaders'

The third image is projected.
Silence is kept.
Endue thy ministers with righteousness.
And make thy chosen people joyful.

4   Image: sick / homeless person
     Caption: '. . . for those in special need'

The fourth image is projected.
Silence is kept.
O Lord, save thy people.
And bless thine inheritance.

5   Image: war scene
     Caption: '. . . for the peace of the
     world'

The fifth image is projected.
Silence is kept.
Give peace in our time, O Lord.
**Because there is none other that fighteth
for us,
but only thou, O God.**

6   Image: human face
     Caption: '. . . for ourselves'

The sixth image is projected.
Silence is kept.
O God, make clean our hearts within us.
And take not thy Holy Spirit from us.

A service for World Human Rights Day

Peter Moger and Ally Barrett

The Revd Ally Barrett is Vicar of Buckden and The Offords and a Vocations Adviser in the Diocese of Ely. Prior to this she was Assistant Curate at Godmanchester, where I (Peter Moger) was Vicar. Ally and I have worked together on a variety of liturgical and musical projects.

Context

This service was held in response to a request from local groups of Amnesty International and of the United Nations Association who wished to celebrate the 55th anniversary of the United Nations Universal Declaration of Human Rights.

It is cast in the typical *Common Worship* fourfold shape and follows the basic framework and requirements of A Service of the Word, though texts are drawn from both within and beyond *Common Worship*. As this service was not held on a Sunday, but on a weekday evening, no Affirmation of Faith was included. The prayers of Penitence were adapted from a worship resource from the Churches' National Housing Coalition and recast into the shape of a *Kyrie* Confession. The Amnesty and UNA groups wanted to include certain non-biblical readings as part of the worship. During the planning, it was decided that these would feature in the third section of the service (Response to God's Word) as contemporary reflections on the challenge to justice that had been heard in the Gospel reading. These reflective readings were interspersed with periods of silence and short pieces of music.

The layout of the space and symbolic action are crucial to this service. Two artefacts are of particular importance:

- The Amnesty Candle (which is made from a large candle encased in twisted barbed wire) is a focal point for the entire liturgy. From its entrance at the Gathering to its use to light smaller candles at the Sending Out, it serves as a reminder of Christ the Light who shines in the darkness, but whom the darkness cannot overcome (cf. John 1.5).
- The second artefact is a large cage – made of wood or metal – which needs to occupy a central location so that it is visible for the entire service. Representing the continual plight of prisoners of conscience, the cage acts as a focus during the Prayers of Penitence (see below) and as a constant reminder throughout the service of the Gospel imperative to seek justice.

The service

The following Introduction was printed on the inside cover of the Order of Service.[48]

This month sees the 55th anniversary of the United Nations Universal Declaration of Human Rights – adopted and proclaimed by the General Assembly of the United Nations on 10th December 1948, a day which is now celebrated annually as World Human Rights Day. The declaration is not merely one more treaty among others, nor simply another piece of paper beloved of governments and diplomats destined to gather dust. The International Covenants on Economic, Social and Cultural Rights and on Civil and Political Rights embody the Universal Declaration of Human Rights. They enshrine in international law the determination to eradicate the evils of torture and the imprisonment of the innocent. In so doing, they mirror in human law the law of God, and the love of God for all people.

In this service, we focus in particular on the millions of men, women and children who live in fear of armed violence, due to an arms trade that is out of control. Every year half a million people die because of the unregulated trade in weapons. Every minute someone dies. In this celebration of the anniversary of this Declaration, we give thanks to God, and also pray earnestly for its full and proper implementation throughout the world.

¶ Gathering in God's Presence

HYMN: *God of freedom, God of justice* (Tune: *Picardy*) (CP 447, CAHON 224, CH4 263)

During the hymn the United Nations Association Standard is received and the Amnesty International Candle is lit.

BIDDING

Minister	The light and peace of Jesus Christ be with you all
All	**and also with you.**

Minister   We have gathered this evening as sisters and brothers of one human family under God
to affirm our belief in the God-given right of human dignity.

We give thanks for the United Nations Universal Declaration of Human Rights, and we pray for its proper implementation throughout the world.
We also remember before God the work of Amnesty International, and the United Nations Association, and especially the local groups represented here.
So let us pray for the coming of God's kingdom in the words our Saviour gave us.

All   **Our Father, who art in heaven . . .**

ACT OF PENITENCE

Minister   Let us confess to God the sins and shortcomings of the world;
its pride, its selfishness, its greed;
its evil divisions and hatreds.
Let us confess our share in what is wrong,
and our failure to establish that peace and justice
which God wills for all his children.

CWT&S (Remembrance Sunday), p. 582

The congregation is invited to take their piece of red wool and, in silence, tie it onto the cage which occupies the centre of the worship space.

Voice 1	You asked for our hands, that you might use them for your purpose;
Voice 2	We gave them for a moment, then withdrew them, for the work was hard.
Minister	Lord, have mercy.*
All	**Lord, have mercy.**

Voice 1	You asked for our mouths, to speak out against injustice;
Voice 2	We gave you a whisper, that we might not be accused.
Minister	Lord, have mercy.
All	**Lord, have mercy.**

Voice 1	You asked for our eyes, to see the pain of poverty;
Voice 2	We closed them, for we did not want to see.
Minister	Christ, have mercy.
All	**Christ, have mercy.**

Voice 1	You asked for our ears, that we might hear the cries of the oppressed;
Voice 2	We did not listen, for it was too hard.
Minister	Christ, have mercy.
All	**Christ, have mercy.**

Voice 1	You asked for our lives, that you might work through us;
Voice 2	We gave you a small part, that we might not get too involved.
Minister	Lord, have mercy.
All	**Lord, have mercy.**

Voice 1	Forgive us for the times we have washed our hands of people,
Voice 2	when we have walked away when they needed us, and offered half measure.
Minister	Lord, have mercy.
All	**Lord, have mercy.**

Adapted from *For the sake of Justice*,
Churches' National Housing Coalition, 1995

The Amnesty Candle is placed next to the cage.

Minister   May the God of love and power
forgive us and free us from our sins,
heal and strengthen us by his Spirit,
and raise us to new life in Christ our Lord.
Amen.

TAIZÉ CHANT: *Bless the Lord, my soul*

¶ God's Word: A Call to Justice

SCRIPTURE READING: Matthew 25.34-45

After the reading, silence is kept and the following response is used:

> I will meditate on your commandments
> **and contemplate your ways.**

Psalm 119.15

SONG: *Christ be our light (Bernadette Farrell)* (CG 21, CH4 543, TS 1409)

SHORT ADDRESS

¶ Responding to God's Word

Response to God's word is made first through a series of short (non-biblical) prose and poetry readings interspersed with periods of silence and instrumental music.

PRAYERS

The Iona chant 'Kindle a flame' (CAON 932, HSNW 135A, SG 658) is sung to introduce the prayers and is repeated after each petition.

After each petition, a candle is lit from the Amnesty Candle and is placed around the cage.

Leader   For the work of Amnesty International,
the United Nations Association and all who strive for freedom,
peace and justice, let us pray to the Lord . . .
All   **Kindle a flame . . .**

Leader   For all in positions of leadership throughout the world,

for our Queen and Members of Parliament,
let us pray to the Lord . . .

All   **Kindle a flame . . .**

Leader   For those places where the Declaration of Human Rights is not
upheld,
and where injustice and corruption are rife,
let us pray to the Lord . . .

All   **Kindle a flame . . .**

Leader   For all held as political prisoners,
those suffering torture and all whose humanity is debased,
let us pray to the Lord . . .

All   **Kindle a flame . . .**

Leader   For those facing execution, those who have been forgotten, or
who have disappeared,
let us pray to the Lord . . .

All   **Kindle a flame . . .**

Leader   For all who have died as a result of injustice and for all who
have gone before us in the struggle for human rights,
let us pray to the Lord . . .

All   **Kindle a flame . . .**

Minister   Almighty Father, you are love,
and see all the suffering, injustice and misery which reign in this
world.
Look with mercy, we pray, upon the poor,
   the oppressed and all who are heavy laden.
Fill our hearts with deep compassion for those who suffer,
and hasten the coming of your kingdom of justice and truth,
through Jesus Christ our Lord.
Amen.

¶ Sending Out

THE BLESSING AND SHARING OF THE LIGHT

The minister stands before the Amnesty Candle.

Minister   Jesus Christ is the light of the world:
All   **a light no darkness can quench.**

Minister   The light and peace of Jesus Christ be with you all
All   **and also with you.**

Minister   Blessed are you, Sovereign God, our light and our salvation;
to you be glory and praise for ever!

May we who walk in the light of your presence
acclaim your Christ, risen, victorious,
as he banishes all darkness from our hearts and minds,
and praise you, Father, Son and Holy Spirit:

All   **Blessed be God for ever.**

*During the following chants, the congregation is invited to come forwards
and light their small candles from the Amnesty Candle.*

TAIZÉ CHANTS: *The Lord is my light* and *Stay with us, O Lord Jesus Christ*

Minister   Lord of light,
may these candles be to those in darkness a sign of hope,
may they inspire the powerful to act with justice and mercy,
and may they remind each of us of our calling
to shine as lights in the world,
through Jesus Christ, the one true Light.
Amen.

HYMN: *Jesus Christ is waiting* (Tune: *Noel Nouvelet*) (CG 67, CH4 360,
CAON 349, SG 624, SOF 1381, TS 1360)

BLESSING AND DISMISSAL

Priest   God whose holy name defies our definition,
but whose will is known in freeing the oppressed,
make you to be one with all who cry for justice;
that those who speak your praise may struggle for your truth;
and the blessing of God almighty,
the Father, the Son and the Holy Spirit,
be among you and remain with you now and always.
Amen.

Minister   For all that has been – thanks!
All   **For all that shall be – yes!**

Go in the light and peace of Christ.
Thanks be to God.

Notes to the service
* a sung *Kyrie* may be used, The *Ghanaian Kyrie* (*Lambeth Praise*, 2008,
p. 181) is particularly appropriate.

All-age liquid worship for Mothering Sunday

Tim Lomax

Background

'One size fits all' may be OK for T-shirts but it doesn't really work for a Mothering Sunday service. This occasion is one of the most challenging for which to plan worship; within any congregation there is an incredible diversity of needs and experiences to accommodate. Catering for them effectively within a 'one size fits all' service in which everyone does the same thing at the same time is well-nigh impossible. A celebratory act of worship can alienate those who are grieving, but a more sombre service might exclude those who are celebrating. Trying to include space for both is tricky.

'Liquid worship' – in a nutshell, 'a flexible form of worship in which individuals are free to combine the different elements of worship into their own preferred journeys'[49] – can help reach the parts that 'one size fits all' services can't reach:

- It provides a flexible worship environment made up of optional zones for prayer or personal response.
- It increases the potential to provide meaningful spiritual encounters by celebrating diversity.
- It allows individuals to be deliberate in their choice of worship activities and opens up opportunities for worship appropriate for particular people at that particular time.
- In addition, the variety of worship stations offered provides activities to suit differences in learning preference, experience, age and circumstance.

Context

Having realized over the years that 'one size' seldom fits all for Mothering Sunday, St John's decided to include 'liquid worship' as a substantial element of their all-age service on this day. The service followed the basic format of A Service of the Word and either side of the liquid worship it was topped and tailed with more conventional sections in which everyone was engaged in the same activity.

All words, images and movie clips were projected onto screens. The liquid worship stations were planned and led by different members of the congregation: this increased creativity, spread the workload and involved people who would otherwise have been reluctant to lead 'up front'.

As usual, many visitors joined the mix of young families, teenagers and grandparents. Families and friendship groups were encouraged to journey around the stations together and conversation was welcomed. Prayer ministry was offered at one of the stations. As worshippers engaged with the stations the number of pastoral conversations which were sparked was very noticeable – something which would not normally have taken place within worship. Many of those visiting commented that they found the worship very 'real' and 'down to earth', and how helpful this was. One person admitted surprise: they had expected a service which made 'little connection with my life'. A number of people also reflected on how a sense of community was heightened during liquid worship. And as they reviewed the service, St John's wondered whether, just as with the Trinity, diversity might lie at the heart of genuine community.

The service

Before the service

The congregation was welcomed informally and notices were given (the spoken words being reinforced by a PowerPoint presentation)

¶ The Gathering

Minister	We are here to worship	*(Hands up)*
	We are here to pray	*(Hands together)*
	We are here to listen	*(Hands behind ears)*
	We are here to praise	*(Hands move from lips)*
	We are here as God's family	*(Family sign)*
	We are here to meet God	*(Hands clasped)*

© Nick Harding[50]

SONG: *Our God is a great big God* (SOF 2004, TS 1475)

PRAYERS OF PENITENCE

Minister   We come to God as one from whom no secrets are hidden,
to ask for his forgiveness and peace.

Lord Jesus, you wept over the sins of your city.
On our city:
Lord, have mercy.
All   **Lord, have mercy.**

Lord Jesus, you heal the wounds of sin and division, jealousy and bitterness.
On us:
Christ, have mercy.
All   **Christ, have mercy.**

Lord Jesus, you bring pardon and peace to the sinner.
Grant us peace:
Lord, have mercy.

All　　　**Lord, have mercy.**

May the God of love
bring *us* back to himself,
forgive *us our* sins,
and assure *us* of his eternal love
in Jesus Christ our Lord.
Amen.

NPFW, p. 94

TAKE IT ON BOARD

A movie clip was shown, an extract from *Charlotte's Web,* a classic story of
loyalty, trust and sacrifice in which a very small pig called Wilbur discovers
the powerful bond of friendship with Charlotte the spider who shows him
extraordinary care and love. This led into an encouragement of the
congregation to do three things during the worship:

1. to thank God for the special people in their lives (including mothers
   who have loved us like Charlotte by showing loyalty, trust and
   sacrifice);
2. to be honest if there is sadness because they have not experienced
   this sort of love or had the opportunity to offer it to others;
3. to be open to God's love shown through the loyalty, trust and
   sacrifice of Jesus.

HYMN: *Great is thy faithfulness*

COLLECT

God of love,
passionate and strong,
tender and careful:
watch over us and hold us
all the days of our life;
through Jesus Christ our Lord.
Amen.

CWCPC, p. 29

¶ The Liturgy of the Word

GOSPEL READING – John 11.1-7 and 17-44

SHORT TALK (5 mins) – illustrated with PowerPoint presentation

AFFIRMATION OF FAITH

Do you believe and trust in God the Father,
source of all being and life,

the one for whom we exist?
We believe and trust in him.

Do you believe and trust in God the Son,
who took our human nature,
died for us and rose again?
We believe and trust in him.

Do you believe and trust in God the Holy Spirit,
who gives life to the people of God
and makes Christ known in the world?
We believe and trust in him.

This is the faith of the Church.
This is our faith.
We believe and trust in one God,
Father, Son and Holy Spirit. Amen.

CWMV, p. 144

¶ Response to the Word

LIQUID WORSHIP STATIONS

7 liquid worship stations were set up. The congregation was given the
following instructions:

---

1   **Thank you** – Daffodils

Write or draw a thank you note on a luggage tag and attach it to a daffodil. Either
place the daffodil in the vase or give it to the person you are thanking.

2   **Hope** – plant a seed

What is it that you hope for?
Write or draw it as a prayer on the sticky label and attach it to a seed pot. Using your
hands place the compost in the pot and then plant a seed. Take the pot home, water
the seed, pray and watch as your seed of hope grows.

3   **Remembering** – memory jars

Who would you like to remember?
Using the coloured salt (salt mixed with coloured chalks) make up layers of colour
within your glass jar. Each layer can represent an aspect of the character of the
person you are remembering (e.g. yellow for sunshine personality, red for fiery
temper) or a memory you shared together. When you have done this, write what
each colour stands for on the label and attach it to the jar.

4   **Loss** – tear drops on the cross

What or who have you lost?
The death of a loved one, the loss of a dream or your health, the end of a

relationship. We grieve each loss we face. Be honest about your loss, talk to God about it in the quiet and ask him to remain faithful to you in it. Afterwards attach a tear to the wooden cross to symbolize your prayer that God will be in it with you.

5 **Celebrations** – making a champagne picture from celebration

6 **Prayer** – praying for Mums in distress

Think of Mums facing a particular difficulty at this time (have information on hand e.g. pictures, stories). What organizations are helping them?
How can we help?
Light a candle for the Mums you have been thinking of.
Think about one thing you can do to help.

7 **Prayer ministry**

A member of the prayer ministry team will be glad to listen to you and pray with you.

The congregation then gathered together again:

- There was a brief look at what had been done or made.
- People were asked if anyone wanted to share something about what they had experienced in the worship.
- There was an acknowledgement of the different responses that had been made at the worship stations. The validity of each of these responses was affirmed and offered to God as the one who cares and meets us in them.

SONG: *Faithful one, so unchanging* (CMP 825, SG 547, SOF 89, TS 89)

THE LORD'S PRAYER

¶ The Dismissal

Final notices were given about post-service Prayer Ministry and refreshments (a warning that Dads would be serving drinks and the cakes they had made!)

CONCLUDING PRAYER

Lord God,
as we go from here we ask that you go with us.
Be with us at home, at school, at work,
Speak to us in the noise and in the quiet.
Walk with us on our journey through life.

BLESSING and DISMISSAL

> The almighty and merciful Lord,
> Father, Son, and Holy Spirit,
> bless us and keep us.
> **Amen.**

> Go in peace to love and serve the Lord.
> **In the name of Christ.**
> **Amen.**

FINAL SONG: *Let everything that has breath praise the Lord*

After-school club worship: a midweek Fresh Expression

Tim Stratford

The Revd Dr Tim Stratford is Team Rector of Kirkby in the Diocese of Liverpool, a large outer-urban parish with a population of 40,000. He is a member of the General Synod, the Liturgical Commission, of the Group for the Renewal of Worship and of the Council of Praxis. He has supplied the following notes on the context of the service.

Context

St Chad's Church in Kirkby is on a road between two primary schools and is surrounded by parents' cars at the beginning and end of each day. This makes access to the church difficult for events at that time of day so the established pattern has been for the church to be closed. On a Sunday, when the church is regularly open, this is a quiet spot where only church attenders and dog walkers are to be found.

Recently the church has decided to open its doors for worship every Tuesday after school. Tea and coffee, soft drinks, biscuits and cake are served from 3.15 p.m. Hospitality before worship rather than afterwards makes it easy for parents and children to arrive at the ragged end of a school day. Worship begins at 3.45. A themed craft or wide-game activity is also laid on throughout the refreshment half hour and this leads into the worship. Children and their parents turn up throughout the half hour as school classes finish.

The worship itself lasts only half an hour and takes place in the chancel of the church. This has quite a large floor area with choir stall running its length on either side. Children tend to gather on the floor, some use hassocks as seat cushions, and adults sit in the stalls. Limited liturgical texts, song words and audio-visuals are presented using a large screen – there are no books or papers. The worship space is attractive and dominated by an arresting Henry Holliday ceramic reredos.

Worship

The structure of the worship is very simple:

- link with pre-worship activity
- gathering rite
- song
- hearing what the Bible says
- song
- reflecting on what the Bible says
- the Lord's Prayer
- dismissal rite.

This structure interprets the basic framework of ASOTW in a way which fits the context. The congregation is gathered, the Bible is read and reflected on, there is prayer and a dismissal. The Gathering and the Dismissal change with each season of the Christian year; over the course of a year they will have introduced many Church of England core texts, responses and rituals. The intention is to help Tuesday worshippers form the same liturgical memory as those who worship on a Sunday, although the musical repertoire and experience of church as a social space will be radically different. After-school church is not thought of as being a pale imitation of Sunday church or a way into Sunday church. It is church. St Chad's intends to grow Christian disciples who worship on Tuesdays and who are every bit as strong as those who worship on a Sunday. The following table shows how liturgical texts in the Gathering and the Dismissal are organized according to season.

Season	Gathering	Dismissal
Autumn Term		
Ordinary Time	The Peace	The Grace
Advent	Prayers of penitence	Seasonal solemn blessing
Spring Term		
Christmas/Epiphany	Lighting baptismal candle and prayers of intercession	'Lighten our Darkness . . .' 'Go in the light and peace of Christ . . .'
Ordinary Time	The Peace	The Grace
Lent	Prayers of penitence	'The peace of God . . . blessing . . .' 'Go in the Peace of Christ . . .'
Summer Term		
Easter	'The Lord be with you . . .' Affirmation of faith	'Go in peace to love and serve the Lord. Alleluia! . . .'
Ordinary Time	The Peace	The Grace

The Lord's Prayer is prayed before the Dismissal every week. The two elements of Bible reading and reflection vary in style. Sometimes the reading is done by youngsters, perhaps four or five using a sentence each, sometimes it is dramatized by a minister involving children, sometimes it is presented in Godly Play style. The reflection can involve games, quizzes, simple crafts or other all-age sermon approaches. The reading is normally derived from the Sunday Principal Service Lectionary and is normally the Gospel. In Ordinary Time a series based on an Old or New Testament character or incident has been stitched together. A small group of parents meeting on a termly basis helps plan this and is also a fertile source of ideas for craft activities, games and quizzes.

This is a work in progress seeking to form Christian disciples among children and adults outside the context of Sunday morning worship but using the same structural building blocks. The provision of A Service of the Word has enabled us to hold worship which is appropriate for our congregation while remaining recognizably Anglican. In time St Chad's hopes to explore how sacramental worship might be built into this pattern too.

The case studies in this chapter have shown that the authorized structure of ASOTW is one which can easily be applied across a wide range of contexts and traditions: to help create services ranging from an 'enhanced' BCP Evensong to liquid worship.

In each case, the use of the structure gives to the service a recognizable framework which helps worshippers take part in a journey as they

- gather
- hear the words of Scripture
- respond, and
- are sent for mission.

The content, however, differs vastly from one service to another. This diversity within given boundaries expresses the heart of the *Common Worship* concept: of worship which connects with the local context while remaining true to its Anglican roots.

6

Case studies: Holy Communion

'One size does not fit all.' Nowhere is this seen more clearly than in this chapter in which we see a variety of creative approaches to the celebration of Holy Communion. Each of them uses the framework either of Holy Communion Order One or of A Service of the Word with a Celebration of Holy Communion. The examples cover a broad range of worshipping situations and traditions – from the fresh expression 'Messy Church' to 'mainstream' Sunday worship. The celebration of Holy Communion lies at the heart of Christian worship – these examples give a flavour of the flexibility that is possible with *Common Worship*.

- The risen Jesus meets us in the word: A Eucharist for Eastertide

Peter Moger and Peter Craig-Wild present a service for a main Sunday celebration of Holy Communion into which seasonal and thematic resources from across the *Common Worship* library are woven.

- Holy Communion in the Charismatic Evangelical tradition

Tim Lomax uses the structure of A Service of the Word with a Celebration of Holy Communion to create an exciting blend of renewal worship and Anglican liturgical structure. The two are not mutually exclusive!

- 'Messy Communion'

Lucy Moore, from 'Messy Church' writes about a recent 'experimental Eucharist' and of the challenges of staging a eucharistic service for a congregation unused to 'traditional church'.

- Harvest Festival Holy Communion in school

Carl Turner explains how, in a school context, the structure of A Service of the Word with a Celebration of Holy Communion provides the basis for a harvest thanksgiving celebration which involves the whole school community.

- Holy Communion in a nursing home or hospital

Kate Lomax, a hospital chaplain, argues for familiarity and simplicity in liturgy when worshipping with the sick.

The risen Jesus meets us in the word: A Eucharist for Eastertide

Peter Craig-Wild / Peter Moger

The Revd Peter Craig-Wild is Team Rector of Maltby in the Diocese of Sheffield and a Member of the Liturgical Commission. Prior to this he was Team Rector of Mirfield and an Honorary Canon of Wakefield Cathedral.

Background

This service is adapted from one in a series featured in the second volume of *Together for a Season (Lent, Holy Week, Easter).*[51] Here, each Eucharist explores the idea that 'The risen Jesus meets us . . .' This particular service is designed for the main Sunday service on the Sixth Sunday of Easter in Years A and B or the Fifth Sunday of Easter in Year C, when the *Common Worship* Principal Service Lectionary Readings are as follows:

Year A	Year B	Year C
(Easter 6)	*(Easter 6)*	*(Easter 5)*
Acts 17.22-31	**Isaiah 55.1-11**	Acts 11.1-18
1 Peter 3.13-22	Acts 10.44-48	Revelation 21.1-6
John 14.15-21	John 15.9-17	**John 13.31-35**
'If you love me you will keep my commandments'	'My word shall not return to me empty'	'I give you a new commandment'

The service explores the idea that, as the Scriptures are read during the Easter season, we come face to face with the transforming reality of the risen Jesus. The service would also be suitable for use on Bible Sunday or on any occasion when the Scriptures are the particular focus of the worship, in which case the appropriate readings from the Principal Service Lectionary would be substituted.

The service

¶ The Gathering

The ministers gather together with

- *The Easter candle (carried by two people)*
- *A large Bible or Book of the Gospels*

The person carrying the Bible lifts it high and says

Your word is a lantern to our feet
All **and a light upon our path.**

An Easter hymn is sung.

The ministers enter with the Easter Candle and Bible held high.

If the layout of the worship area allows, the procession stops in the middle of the congregation.

People are encouraged to gather around the Bible.

GREETING

The president says

Grace, mercy and peace from God our Father and the Lord Jesus
   Christ be with you
and also with you

Alleluia! Christ is risen.
He is risen indeed. Alleluia!

PRAISE

The person / people carrying the Bible hold (s) it up high and someone next to it leads the following acclamation

Blessed are you, Lord our God.
How sweet are your words to the taste,
sweeter than honey to the mouth.
Blessed be God (for ever).

How precious are your commands for our life,
more than the finest gold in our hands.
Blessed be God (for ever).

How marvellous is your will for the world,
unending is your love for the nations.
Blessed be God (for ever).

Our voices shall sing of your promises
and our lips declare your praise.
Blessed be God Father, Son and Holy Spirit.
Blessed be God for ever.

Thanksgiving for the Word, CWDP, p. 304

PRAYERS OF PENITENCE

A minister says

When we cry out to the Lord in our trouble,
he will deliver us from our distress.

God will bring us out of darkness
and out of the shadow of death.

Your word convicts us:
all have sinned and fallen short of the glory of God.
Lord, have mercy.
Lord, have mercy.

Your word commands us:
repent, and believe the good news.
Christ, have mercy.
Christ, have mercy.

Your word assures us:
Christ Jesus came into the world to save sinners.
Lord, have mercy.
Lord, have mercy.

The president says

May the Father forgive *us*
by the death of his Son
and strengthen *us*
to live in the power of the Spirit
all *our* days.
Amen.

Let us give thanks to the Lord for his goodness,
and the wonders he does for his children.

Let us offer him sacrifices of thanksgiving
and tell of his acts with shouts of joy.

cf Psalm 107
No. 4 of Forms of Penitence, CWDP, p. 95
Kyrie sentences from CWT&S, p. 529

Gloria in excelsis, an Easter hymn or a song of praise is sung.

The Bible is placed in a prominent position.

THE COLLECT

In Eastertide:

Risen Christ,
by the lakeside you renewed your call to your disciples:

help your Church to obey your command
and draw the nations to the fire of your love,
to the glory of God the Father.
Amen.

CWCPC, p. 40

On Bible Sunday:

Merciful God,
teach us to be faithful in change and uncertainty,
that trusting in your word
and obeying your will
we may enter the unfailing joy of Jesus Christ our Lord.
Amen.

CWCPC, p. 68

¶ The Liturgy of the Word

READING FROM ACTS (Years A / C) or the OLD TESTAMENT (Year B)

A hymn or song may be sung.

The reader picks up the Bible and carries it to the middle of the congregation.

GOSPEL READING

Jesus Christ is risen from the dead.
Alleluia.

He has defeated the powers of death.
Alleluia.

Jesus turns our sorrow into dancing.
Alleluia.

He has the words of eternal life.
Alleluia.

CWT&S, p. 431

Hear the Gospel of our Lord Jesus Christ according
to John.
Glory to you, O Lord.

The Gospel for the day is read.

This is the Gospel of the Lord.
Praise to you, O Christ.

SERMON

A sermon or talk follows, or people might be encouraged to share their favourite Bible passages or stories – or they could be given a list from which to choose.

AFFIRMATION OF FAITH

Let us declare our faith
   in the resurrection of our Lord Jesus Christ.

> **Christ died for our sins**
> **in accordance with the Scriptures;**
> **he was buried;**
> **he was raised to life on the third day**
> **in accordance with the Scriptures;**
> **afterwards he appeared to his followers,**
> **and to all the apostles:**
> **this we have received,**
> **and this we believe.**
> **Amen.**

CWMV, p. 147
cf 1 Corinthians 15.3-7

PRAYERS OF INTERCESSION

The minister introduces a time of active prayer.

The congregation may be given cards on which they write or draw subjects for prayer.

When they are ready they bring them forwards and place them around the Bible.

A chant such as 'O Lord hear my prayer' may be sung.

When everyone has placed their prayer cards around the Bible the minister concludes with a short prayer.

> Faithful God,
> let your word be the treasure of our hearts,
> that we may delight in your truth
> and walk in the glorious liberty of your Son Jesus Christ.
> **Amen.**

CWDP, p. 830

¶ The Liturgy of the Sacrament

THE PEACE

> God calls us to life.
> **In his word is our life.**
>
> God calls us to peace.
> **In his word is our peace.**
>
> The peace of the risen Lord be with you
> **and also with you.**

A hymn or song is sung as the table is prepared.

The table may be prepared from scratch with different people bringing in the altar cloth, candles, corporal, paten, chalice, bread, wine, water, etc.

An authorized Eucharistic Prayer is used.

THE LORD'S PRAYER

> Trusting in God's word,
> let us pray as our Saviour taught us
> **Our Father in heaven . . .**

BREAKING OF THE BREAD

The word of God in Scripture has been broken open for us.

(Now) . . . *the president breaks the bread . . .*

> We break this bread to share in the body of Christ.
> **Though we are many we are one body**
> **because we all share in the one bread.**

The ministers and people receive Communion.

POST COMMUNION PRAYER

Silence is kept.

> **Almighty God,**
> **we thank you for the gift of your holy word.**
> **May it be a lantern to our feet,**
> **a light upon our paths,**
> **and a strength to our lives.**
> **Take us and use us**

> **to love and serve all people**
> **in the power of the Holy Spirit**
> **and in the name of your Son,**
> **Jesus Christ our Lord. Amen.**

¶ The Dismissal

A hymn is sung, during which the ministers move to the door from where the
Dismissal Gospel is to be read. The procession may be led by the Easter
Candle and the large Bible which is held high.

ACCLAMATION

> The Word of life which was from the beginning
> **we proclaim to you.**

> The darkness is passing away and the true light is already shining;
> **the Word of life which was from the beginning.**

> That which we heard, which we saw with our eyes, and touched with
> our hands,
> **we proclaim to you.**

> For our fellowship is with the Father, and with his Son, Jesus Christ
> our Lord.
> **The Word of life, which was from the beginning, we proclaim**
> **to you.**

Thanksgiving for the Word, CWMV, p. 46

DISMISSAL GOSPEL

> Hear the Gospel of our Lord Jesus Christ according to John.
> **Glory to you, O Lord.**

> Jesus said to the Jews who had believed in him,
> **'If you continue in my word, you are truly my disciples;**
> **and you will know the truth, and the truth will make you**
> **free.'**

John 8.31-32

> This is the Gospel of the Lord.
> **Praise to you, O Christ.**

BLESSING

> [Alleluia! Christ is risen.
> **He is risen indeed. Alleluia!]**

May the risen Christ, the Word of God,
fill you with boldness to proclaim the gospel;
and the blessing . . .

DISMISSAL

Blessed are those who hear the word of God and obey it.

Go in the peace of the risen Christ.
Thanks be to God.

Holy Communion in the Charismatic Evangelical tradition

Tim Lomax

The Revd Tim Lomax is Assistant Curate of St Philip's, Penn Fields, Wolverhampton and a member of the Liturgical Commission. Prior to ordination he was a musician and Worship Pastor at Holy Trinity Church, Cambridge. He has supplied the following notes on the background to this service.

Background

Are we tired of the *basics* range and longing to *taste the difference* when it comes to celebrating Holy Communion? Are we weary of worship that lacks flavour, nutrition and visual impact?

Maybe it's time to rediscover an approach which *Common Worship* has at its core. This approach encourages imaginative engagement in worship which can in turn open the way for people in a variety of circumstances to experience the love of God in Jesus Christ in the life and power of the Holy Spirit. However, this approach to worship is all too often ignored. A substantial number of churches within the evangelical tradition are fearful of liturgical texts and indeed of Anglican-shaped liturgy. The Holy Communion service is frequently stripped of most of its form and shape. This is probably because some see more traditional Church of England liturgy (the shapes and the texts) as a 'prison' restricting creativity, freedom and even the work of the Spirit.

This negative view of shapes and texts has arisen in part through the poor use of liturgy in the past. People remember when services played liturgical texts 'by the book'. The view still hangs around today that a 'proper' service is one which uses 'correct liturgy' rather than looking at the *way* the liturgy is used. This is, understandably, off-putting to many. However, such an approach owes far too much to a dated understanding of Anglican worship in which a service is 'read' from beginning to end (see Chapter 1, pages 7–8), and totally fails to capture the intention of *Common Worship* – to encourage context and creativity. We should be more concerned, not with using correct liturgy, but with using liturgy correctly.

So why not use *Common Worship* as it was intended – as scaffolding, a structure within which something creative and beautiful can be built which is tailor-made for our local context? Liturgical texts and structures then become frameworks to enable freedom. Within these time-honoured shapes, imaginative and contemporary worship can be created – worship that has the potential to lead people in to the heart of the love of God.

Essentially, the *Common Worship* Order for Holy Communion (Order One) follows the basic shape of a meal:

- gathering as community (friends at the table)
- engaging with God's word (receiving nourishment)

- celebrating around the table (breaking bread and pouring wine)
- and taking the gospel to the world (sharing the food we have enjoyed).

Within this basic shape there is great scope for liturgical creativity and freedom. This structure is the scaffolding within which vital building blocks can be put together to create vibrant, compelling worship for the contemporary church.

The following approaches to worship are the building-blocks which help form a healthy church community:

- **seeking genuinely Trinitarian worship** (worshipping the Father, with and through the Son in the power of the Holy Spirit);
- **facilitating worship that is gospel-rich** (responding to all that God has done through Christ);
- **connecting with culture** (worship sparking within our world today);
- **deepening relationships** (worship events encouraging friendship);
- **showing generosity** (demonstrating the grace of God in community);
- **involving all** (celebrating diversity – the range of learning preferences, faith journeys, ethnicity and circumstance);
- **being creative** (remixing the traditional, pioneering the new);
- **maintaining imaginative engagement with *Common Worship* values and frameworks** (realizing the wealth our liturgical heritage affords us);
- **journeying as sacramental community** (building essential expressions of Christian life into community);
- **interceding for the world**, and
- **absorbing and internalising core Christian texts** (e.g. the Lord's Prayer, *Kyrie*, the Grace, dialogues between the minister and congregation).

Adopting these approaches impacts on every aspect of a service – the liturgies, music, style and visual elements chosen. These building blocks are vital as they help determine the extent to which communities are being formed and transformed. They also help ensure that *Common Worship* is used to its full potential as we take full advantage of the resources it contains. But how we work out these approaches, putting together the building blocks within the scaffolding of the liturgy is down to us, *our* creativity and *our* context – that's the beauty of *Common Worship*!

So how might the Order One Holy Communion service in *Common Worship* be presented so that it is faithful both to its Anglican roots and to current worshipping practice within the evangelical tradition?

In the opening section of Order One the congregation gathers in **preparation**.

- An opening **hymn or song** is used to draw the community God-wards, to unite in praise and to set the service in the context of God's story of grace through history.

- The **Greeting** (whether a text from the book is used or not) is a simple statement of expectation and a welcome in the Lord's name.
- The **Prayer of Preparation** (the Collect for Purity) may be replaced with a song or an extemporary prayer which demonstrates that the community has gathered in the presence of the Triune God and which invokes the Holy Spirit, asking that hearts may be cleansed and made better able to offer loving worship to God.
- **Prayers of penitence** are printed as part of the Gathering in *Common Worship* (though they may be moved later if desired) because confession and forgiveness stand at the core of the Christian faith. The prayers of penitence help facilitate the lifestyle of repentance, of turning towards God and away from all that competes with him.
  - Texts for the invitation to confession are suggested but the president is free to use seasonal provision, other suitable words or perhaps a song, piece of music or film clip.
  - A variety of options is provided for the prayer of confession (see Chapter 4).
  - The absolution is carefully worded and clearly states God's forgiveness, highlights that authority to absolve comes from him, and demonstrates that repentance can only ever be in response to God's grace.
  - Why not wrap the Confession with a hymn or song, as in the use of verses from *Before the throne of God above* in the sample service below?
- The **Gloria** is a point at which we join in the ancient and ongoing hymn of praise to the Triune God and as such is a wonderfully uplifting response to hearing God's forgiveness. Again, considerable creative licence can be used here as an alternative to the text of the Gloria in Excelsis. Suitable songs or hymns could be used or music played. Or why not commission the music leader or lead worshipper to write a contemporary setting of the Gloria?
- The Gathering is concluded with the **Collect**. This is an ideal time to slot in a time of silence or space for more open worship following sung worship before the president collects or gathers up the prayer and worship of the people. Some might feel it appropriate to give this responsibility to the music leader at this point so that they conclude this section of worship. However, we would suggest that the Collect demonstrates the ministry of the president as the one who draws the congregation into a worshipping community around the Lord's table.
- The elements which make up the Gathering are not separate or unrelated items, but knit together effectively to help God's people begin a significant journey in worship together.

The **Liturgy of the Word** is a core element of Holy Communion. It has of course long been understood that encountering Scripture corporately has an essential role to play in the shaping of Christian community. Demanding patterns of work often make a time for personal devotions and study unrealistic for congregation members. Therefore, engaging with Scripture in gathered worship is crucial to the life of the Church. Evangelicals have traditionally been strong advocates of this view. However, increasingly, evangelical churches are omitting (or at least significantly reducing) the public reading and hearing of Scripture and instead simply engaging with God's word spoken through preaching. While preaching is important, it is essential that it is firmly rooted in the Scriptures and that God's people, gathered for worship, hear the words of the Bible spoken in their midst.

The **Creed** expresses beliefs shared by Christians throughout the world and across all time. It reinforces the fact that Christian faith is not confined to the individual, but shared and lived out in community, and reminds us of the core truths that underpin our faith. Many churches use the Creed creatively, either singing it, saying it while listening to background music, reading it silently (after all, we can sit together in silence and feel connected to each other), chanting it to a dance rhythm, or saying it together before responding through a simple ritual.

Immediate response to God's word does not have to be restricted to the Creed and it often feels a shame at times when it is. Sung worship can be used at this point in the service, as can silent meditation or prayer ministry, to name but a few ideas.

Justin Martyr of Rome records that general prayers were offered at the Eucharist by the gathered people. *Common Worship* simply continues this pattern with the **prayers of intercession**. Once again, we are reminded that faith is not simply an individual matter as we follow the biblical imperatives to bring the needs of others before God in prayer.

The **Peace** acts as a bridge between the Liturgy of the Word and the Liturgy of the Sacrament. It also reinforces the sense of being in a holy fellowship as we come to the Lord's table. The default form of the Peace is often the traditional handshake, or a hug and a kiss if you're lucky. But maybe it is time to reimagine what the Peace could look like today. What other ways are there to demonstrate that we are a holy fellowship, a community at one with each other and the Lord, gathered at his table? Be creative, ask your congregation for ideas.

The **eucharistic prayer** continues the action of Christ at the Last Supper. This is done through the four actions – taking bread and wine, thanking God for them, breaking bread, and sharing bread and wine. Some churches have departed from Anglican practice, have done away with the eucharistic prayer and use instead a few sentences of Scripture. This is again a reaction against the 'straight' use of liturgical texts in which there is little creativity or action and shows a lack of understanding about what is happening at this point in the service. Used as it should be, the eucharistic prayer is an unfolding drama, God's overarching story within which worshippers can see their own story. The telling of the story and the acting of the drama are therefore essential. What could you do in your local context to bring the drama alive? Use the gifts of your congregation, involve all ages in the preparation of the table, sing responses, or why not wrap the eucharistic prayer with a suitable hymn or song (e. g. *Holy, Holy, Holy; Crown him with many crowns;* or Stuart Townend's *Behold the Lamb of God*)? The possibility of using music to underpin the whole prayer, with the congregation joining in from time to time with acclamations, can also be explored. Look for songs which pick up the theme of the *Sanctus* ('Holy, holy, holy Lord . . .') and which might be sung at this point in the prayer. Think about what the president is doing with his / her hands during the prayer – how is the invocation of the Spirit expressed, for instance? And encourage the congregation to pray the prayer with their eyes open!

Many see the giving of communion as an opportunity for more reflective worship and prayer. Sung worship works well here (with well-chosen songs) and prayer ministry could be offered. Sung worship can grow and gather momentum within this section of the worship: as people return to their seats having received bread and wine, the volume increases and in time each member of the community adds his or her voice. A post communion prayer draws this section to a close – once again, a well-chosen song could help facilitate this.

The **Dismissal** rounds off the whole service and is there to make the link between our worship and the missional lifestyle for which we are being commissioned. The blessing (using a given text or *extempore*) demonstrates that the community journeys on with God's blessing, his guarding and his guiding.

Context

St Philip's celebrates Holy Communion at its 10.30 service once a month. It gathers a congregation predominantly made up of young families (about 80 adults and 50 children and young people). The church has been considering the admission of baptized children to Holy Communion and, so as to better inform the church and the PCC discussion, it was decided to spend some time focusing specifically on Holy Communion in its Sunday worship, cell group material and children's church teaching material. This service took place on a Sunday in Ordinary Time, so advantage was taken of the dispensation to depart from an authorized Lectionary, and a thematic Gospel Reading – Luke 22.14–20 – was chosen. The service of Holy Communion that day encapsulated the church's aim in all its worship – to encounter God through services that are all-age, creative, accessible, mission-focused, which build relationships and which aim for quality. A band supplied the music, all words were projected on to the screens, as were film clips, images and PowerPoint (for the notices and the Sermon). To help worshippers follow clearly the structure of the service and to give a sense of navigation within it, a progress bar was used at the foot of the data projector screen.

The service follows the shape of Holy Communion Order One, while making use of the dispensations of A Service of the Word with a Celebration of Holy Communion.

The service

Eucharist: uniting past, present and future

¶ Before the Service

The congregation was welcomed and notices were given
PowerPoint was used to reinforce notices

¶ The Gathering

SONG: *All my days* (CH4 467, CMP 1024, SOF 1158, TS 1105)

GREETING

MOVIE CLIP

The opening scene from *Chocolat* was shown – followed by discussion in small groups, with the following questions being asked:

- Do we need or want God to fling open the doors of our hearts with the wind of his Spirit?
- Why?
- And for what?

PRAYER OF PREPARATION (Collect for Purity)

CWMV, p. 168

SONG: *God, you're so cool*[52]

INFORMAL (extempore) PRAYER FOR CHILDREN – children leave for groups

PRAYERS OF PENITENCE

- Song: *Before the throne of God above* (verses 1 and 2) (CP 283, CH4 466, CMP 975, SG 169, SOF 1187, TS 643)
Musicians continue to play quietly . . .
- Invitation to Confession (CWMV, p. 168)
- Confession (CWMV, p. 169)
- Song: *Before the throne of God above* (verse 3)
Musicians continue to play quietly . . .

109

- Absolution (CWMV, p. 170)

SONGS

- *There is a Redeemer* (CH4 559, CMP 673, CAHON 658, SG 396, SOF 544, TS 492)
- *How great thou art*
- *The splendour of the King* (SOF 2065)

Musicians continue to play quietly . . .

SPACE FOR OPEN WORSHIP

COLLECT *(voice-over)*

> God of constant mercy,
> who sent your Son to save us:
> remind us of your goodness,
> increase your grace within us,
> that our thankfulness may grow,
> through Jesus Christ our Lord.
> **Amen.**

CWCPC, p. 58

¶ The Liturgy of the Word

GOSPEL READING – Luke 22.14-20

SERMON: 'Eucharist – uniting past present and future' (*illustrated with PowerPoint*)

SONG: *As we gather, Father, seal us* (SOF 1717, TS 1134)

AFFIRMATION OF FAITH: *We believe in God the Father* (sung to *Blaenwern*)

CWMV, p. 146

PRAYERS OF INTERCESSION

These were presented as a movie of the past week's news images, with music.

¶ The Liturgy of the Sacrament

THE PEACE

> We are the body of Christ.
> **By one Spirit we were baptized into one body.**

Keep the unity of the Spirit in the bond of peace.
We are bound by the love of Christ.

cf 1 Corinthians 12.13; Ephesians 4.3

The peace of the Lord be always with you
and also with you.

SONG (*during which the Table is prepared*)

Behold the Lamb who bears our sins away (Townend) (verses 1–3) (SOF 1724)
Musicians continue to play quietly . . .

EUCHARISTIC PRAYER E

The Lord be with you
and also with you.

Lift up your hearts.
We lift them to the Lord.

Let us give thanks to the Lord our God.
It is right to give thanks and praise.

It is indeed right and good,
our duty and our salvation
always and everywhere to give you thanks and praise
holy Father, almighty and eternal God,
through Jesus Christ our great high priest.
He offered himself to you as the Lamb without blemish,
the acceptable gift that gives you perfect praise.
At the Last Supper, seated with his apostles,
he left this memorial of his passion
to bring us its saving power until the end of time.
In this great sacrament you feed your people
and strengthen them in holiness,
so that throughout the world the human family
may be enlightened by one faith
and drawn together in one communion of love.
We come to this foretaste of your heavenly banquet
to be transformed by your grace
and restored in the image and likeness of the risen Christ.
Therefore earth unites with heaven
to sing a new song of praise;
we too join with angels and archangels
as they proclaim your glory without end:

CWT&S, p. 518

Musicians lead into song . . .

Song: *Holy is the Lord God almighty*

> Holy, holy,
> Holy is the Lord God Almighty.
> Holy, holy,
> Holy is the Lord God Almighty.
> Who was and is and is to come,
> Who was and is and is to come.
>
> Lift up His name with the sound of singing,
> Lift up His name in all the earth.
> Lift up your voice and give Him glory,
> For He is worthy to be praised.

> Nathan Fellingham, copyright © 1986 Thankyou Music[53]

We praise and bless you, loving Father,
  through Jesus Christ, our Lord; . . .
. . . Through Christ, and with Christ, and in Christ,
in the unity of the Holy Spirit,
all honour and glory are yours, O loving Father,
for ever and ever.
Amen.

Musicians lead into next song . . .

SONG: *Behold the Lamb* (Townend) (verse 4)

Musicians continue to play quietly . . .

THE LORD'S PRAYER

BREAKING OF THE BREAD

> Every time we eat this bread
> and drink this cup,
> **we proclaim the Lord's death**
> **until he comes.**

GIVING OF COMMUNION

SONGS DURING COMMUNION

- *You chose the cross with every breath*
- *We bow down*
- *When I survey the wondrous cross*

POST COMMUNION PRAYER

Holy God,
you have fed us with the body and blood of your Son
by it you nourish our faith,
increase our hope,
and strengthen our love.
May we honour you at school,
at home and at work,
not only with our lips
but in lives dedicated to you.
Amen.

SONG: *Behold the Lamb* (verse 4 and final chorus)

¶ The Dismissal

BLESSING

Christ, who has nourished us with himself the living bread,
make you one in praise and love,
and raise you up at the last day;
and the blessing . . .

CWT&S, p. 519

DISMISSAL

Go in peace to love and serve the Lord.
In the name of Christ. Amen.

'Messy Communion': Holy Communion as part of a Messy Church act of worship

Lucy Moore

Background

Lucy Moore is a professional actor and storyteller and an author and member of the Barnabas Ministry Team of the Bible Reading Fellowship. In 2004 she set up 'Messy Church',[54] a fresh expression at St Wilfrid's, Cowplain, in the Portsmouth Diocese. This attempts to be church for families who might want to meet Jesus, belong to their local church and bring up their children as Christians but can't cope with traditional Sunday morning church services. It takes place once a month and involves creativity, worship and eating together, and has been featured on the Fresh Expressions DVD[55] and written about in *Messy Church: Fresh Ideas for Building a Christ-centred Community*.[56] Lucy has supplied the following notes on the context for this service.[57]

Context

Portsmouth Diocesan Liturgical Group asked the local Messy Churches to organize a Messy Communion at Portsmouth Cathedral in January 2009 as the first of a series of experimental eucharists during the year. One Messy Church had already held a Messy Communion the previous April, so the larger celebration was able to build on the lessons learned from this experience. The main issue for the planning team was trying to find a suitable liturgy for the people for whom Messy Church exists. Messy Church is a form of church centred around the needs of people who don't go to traditional church services. Instead they have grown into a Christian community where worship is based around story, is participative, inclusive, fun, short and relatively informal and where careful consideration is given to the language used to make sure that it is clear without being childish.

When the full texts of *Common Worship* Communion services were examined in the light of the needs of these people some problems were evident. People vary not only in literacy, academic ability and length of attention span, but also in age, learning preferences, motivation for being present and degree of faith development. The Messy Church congregation has not learned to 'behave' in the accepted sense of church behaviour; it is used to a great deal of engagement and participation.

The length of what might be perceived as the 'required' parts of a Communion service threatened to turn it into a something far longer than a usual Messy Church celebration (about fifteen minutes). A full eucharistic liturgy tries to do everything – express what we believe, confess and be absolved, hear the Gospel, remember the death and resurrection of Jesus, commit ourselves to going out to act on this in the world and receiving the

Holy Spirit. For a congregation used to a single theme or story being explored through different media in depth, it was hard to see that the flow of this eucharistic service would make sense. Just one of those elements of the service would normally provide a whole two hours' worth of 'messy' discovery. Asking forgiveness, to take one example, would be a discipline that Messy Church might adopt as its theme for the whole two hour session. This would be explored through craft, story, song, prayer and conversation rather than being touched upon as part of a service focused on a completely different story (in this case, the Last Supper). It is not that Messy Church takes the different parts of the Communion service lightly: it is rather that there is a desperate longing to take every part seriously and make it as accessible and enjoyable and meaningful as possible.

The language of Holy Communion Order One is far more literary, religious and complex than the usual language used at messy celebrations. The length of the eucharistic prayer and the language used could be a 'turn-off' point which would lose the concentration of too many members of the congregation. The sheer number of *words* in the service means that for those who learn best through forms other than language, it can seem rather impoverished. A significant proportion of the service relies on responses that would need to be read, and with a congregation containing many who are pre-literate or functionally illiterate, this also seemed inappropriate. Again, the group wanted desperately to share their love of Holy Communion, rather than insist that barriers were raised against a full enjoyment of the celebration.

Working with the bishop and the diocesan liturgical group, different ways forwards were considered. There was a joy on all sides that the discussion was carried out in a spirit of grace and understanding rather than one of point-scoring or defensiveness. The event began with an hour's activity including a welcome, Gospel story, and a variety of crafts which explored themes of the Eucharist and included intercessory prayer. Many of the crafts were then brought to the holy table for the eucharistic liturgy which followed. There was no written order of service and no seats, simply a gathering around the table in the choir. The celebration was followed by a sit-down meal and far too much cake!

While the liturgy below is far from perfect or finalized, it came from the people and was created for this particular group of people. Perhaps the most telling comment from one of the stewards who had not experienced Messy Church before was a startled: 'But the children were completely engaged all through the communion! They weren't running round the cathedral!' It is debatable whether this was a credit to the way this particular communion service had gone or an indictment of the usual way of doing communion.

The service

During the first part of the event, the congregation had gathered, engaged with and responded to the Gospel and taken part in intercessory prayer – equating to the first three sections of the authorized structure of A Service of the Word with a Celebration of Holy Communion.

The congregation then assembled at the font.

Objects to be used in the celebration were given to members of the congregation (both adults and children) to carry in.

Leader   We're about to celebrate a special meal together, as Jesus' friends have done for thousands of years. We'll start with a sprinkling of water from the font here to remind us of baptism – our own baptism or what baptism means. Can you answer 'We're ready!' to these questions?

Are you ready to remember baptism?

All   We're ready!

The congregation is sprinkled with water from the font.

This section could easily be developed to include the Confession (below), making use of the sprinkling of the water during the words of absolution as a sign of God's forgiveness of sin.

Leader   Now, are you ready to celebrate?
All   We're ready!

Leader   We're about to do what Jesus told us to do to remember him. Are you ready to remember him?
All   We're ready!

Leader   In the name of the Father and the Son and the Holy Spirit, are you ready?
All   We're ready!

Leader   Then let's go!

The song 'We are walking in the light of God' is sung in procession to the table.

The leader invites everyone to hold someone's hand as they come in – a friend or member of your family – so that no one is on their own.

The congregation gathers around the table in a circle.

Leader   The table needs to be got ready for our special remembering meal.
Let's bring up the things we need.

Members of the congregation bring up cup, plate, bread and wine and also the prayers in whatever form they have been prayed earlier.

The leader describes each item briefly and places them on the table.

Leader   And now the table is ready.
              So that we're ready on the inside too, we need to say sorry to
              God for the wrong things we've thought and said and done, and
              all the good things we haven't done.
              In a moment of quiet let's tell God what we're sorry for, and ask
              for his forgiveness.

[PRAYER OF CONFESSION and ABSOLUTION, such as

God our Father,
we come to you in sorrow for our sins.

For turning away from you,
and ignoring your will for our lives;
Lord, have mercy.
Lord, have mercy.

For behaving just as we wish,
without thinking of you;
Christ, have mercy.
Christ, have mercy.

For failing you by what we do,
and think and say;
Lord, have mercy.
Lord, have mercy.

Adapted from NPFW B49

May God our Father forgive *us our* sins
and bring *us* to the fellowship of his table
with his saints for ever.
Amen.]

Leader   We have so much to say thank you for!
              Please say 'thank you Lord' after these short prayers.
              For all your forgiveness,
All   **Thank you, Lord.**

Leader   For all the wonderful things you've done for us,
All   **Thank you, Lord.**

Leader   For making us to be like you,
All   **Thank you, Lord.**

Leader   For mending us whenever we are broken,
All   **Thank you, Lord.**

Leader   For holding our hand as we journey on,
All   **Thank you, Lord.**

Leader   Now we're ready to remember what Jesus has done.

[EUCHARISTIC PRAYER]

Communion is distributed.

A quiet song (either live or on a CD) is played during communion.

Leader	Dear God, for all you give us,
All	**Thank you, Lord.**

Leader	For giving us this family to love and to love us,
All	**Thank you, Lord.**

Leader	For giving us yourself,
All	**Thank you, Lord.**

Leader	Let's say the grace together:	
All	**May the grace of our Lord Jesus Christ**	*hold out hands to receive*
	and the love of God	*cross arms on chest*
	and the fellowship of the Holy Spirit	*hold hands with neighbours*
	be with us all, evermore. Amen!	*Raise hands in the air together*

Leader	And now let's thank God for the tea we're about to eat:
All	**Three, two, one, one, two, three, thank you God for all our tea.**

Leader	Go in peace to love and serve the Lord
All	**In the name of Christ. Amen.**

Copyright © Messy Church 2008

Harvest Festival Holy Communion in school

Carl Turner

The Revd Canon Carl Turner is Precentor of Exeter Cathedral, Chaplain to the General Synod and a member of the Liturgical Commission. He has supplied the following notes on the context for the service.

Context

Exeter Cathedral School is very much a eucharistic community and, in addition to the choristers and boarders who attend the Sunday Eucharist, Holy Communion is celebrated several times a term in the medieval Chapter House which also serves as the school hall. It is a large airy space, brightly lit through two huge east and west windows with decorated tracery. The floor is new, made of polished marble, and the stone benches around the space have new brightly coloured tapestry cushions.

The space is very flexible and allows for children to sit on the floor or on chairs and adults to sit around the outside edge. The normal configuration is a 'horse-shoe' shape which provides a sense of intimacy, the altar and other liturgical items being placed in the central space. The school has a beautiful small wooden altar made by the art department and also a matching paschal candlestick made out of a large branch of a holly tree which is in memory of a chorister who died tragically in 2001. The PA system, which allows for radio microphones as well as standing mics, is a recent installation and speakers are on the walls around the Chapter House. There is a built-in CD player and computers and DVDs can be fed through it to provide excellent sound reproduction. A data projector and laptop are provided on a mobile rack allowing images to be projected directly onto the Chapter House walls or onto a large screen.

School worship is led by lay and ordained people, but with much participation from the pupils. Specifically, whenever a school Eucharist is to be celebrated, the lay chaplain gathers together a particular class or year group to help prepare and plan. Initial planning is made between the Precentor, as priest to the school, and the lay chaplain. Once the basic shape and theme are decided, then the lectionary is agreed and a decision made as to which year group or class should make the detailed preparations. The children are involved in expanding the theme though the preparation of liturgical texts, prayers, readings, music, drama, symbolic action and art as appropriate. The school has very small class sizes and this allows for as few as ten or fifteen children to gather exploring a particular theme, festival or Bible reading. The school is aiming to be awarded eco-status and the children often find ways of connecting the liturgy with the environment and other social contexts. As it is a church school, RE is a core subject in practice and not just in name, and the children regularly reflect on the world around them, including what is happening on the world stage as well as nearer to home. From the Foot and Mouth crisis which affected farmers' children at the school to concern about global warming, the children are encouraged to make connections between their growing spirituality and their sense of being citizens.

The daily act of collective worship also uses, albeit in a simpler way, similar practices and themes so that the school eucharists are seen not as special 'extras' but part of the normal rhythm of prayer for the school community. The daily 'assembly' thus becomes a useful tool for preparing the whole school for liturgical worship; learning new hymns and chants, exploring particular themes and praying together give the children a 'tool bag' which they can draw on as they grow older. One particular example of this tool bag and one often commented on by visitors is the use of silence; the children are used to exercise – sport plays an important part in the life of the school – but they are also used to their spiritual exercises in which they practice being still and meditative.

The regular use of silence and guided prayer has had a profound effect on the liturgical life of the school with the children moving with ease from excitement to stillness and vice versa. After a *Gloria in Excelsis* using clapping and percussion, the children respond to the invitation 'Let us pray' almost immediately. After the preparation of the gifts, which nearly always uses an 'up-beat' song, the children become very still for the eucharistic prayer. As the dominical words are said and the president looks at the children, a profound silence descends upon the Chapter House. Once, a visitor, arriving late, was clearly alarmed by the sight of children being so still and asked the Headmaster, 'What was the matter with the children?' 'They were praying, madam' came the answer! The use of the body to pray is also important and from Reception onwards the children are encouraged to pray with hands extended. As they progress through the school they encounter encouragement to think about posture and breathing. One unforeseen, but marvellous result of this is the way that overseas students from the Far East are able to relate to contemplative prayer. The small number of children from Japan and Thailand use skills they have learned at home and are able to demonstrate them to others.

This particular liturgy was the school's annual Harvest Festival. Through Geography and RE the children had discovered the 'Shelterbox' project supported by Rotary clubs which aims to respond to natural disasters by providing large green plastic boxes filled with enough emergency equipment to keep a family of six alive in harsh conditions for several months. The whole of the Autumn term was spent with sponsored activities and other fund-raising to raise enough for one shelterbox. The Harvest Festival Eucharist was a focal point for encouraging children, staff and parents to take this on board and another speaker came, together with a shelterbox, to speak at the celebration.

The shelterbox was placed in the centre of the liturgical space and opened so that its contents could spill out around the altar. Images of the shelterbox and of natural disasters, to enable people to make connections, were included in the simple order of service. It was intended to be taken home and several pages had line drawings for children to colour later and give an opportunity for discussion with parents. The liturgy was designed to encourage and to look forward; 'shelterbox' became a regular subject for intercessions and featured in the planning for the school end of term carol service – the art department made four banners to explore the theme of refugees using modern-day images from Israel and Palestine. In the end, no fewer than *four* shelterboxes were bought and one of them was blessed at Christmas.

The children explored the Gospel reading that was to be used for this celebration – it was to be very brief and to the point:

> As they went on their way a man said to Jesus, 'I will follow you wherever you go. Jesus said to him, 'Foxes have holes, and birds have nests, but the Son of Man has no place to lie down and rest.' (Luke 9.57–59)

They suggested hymns and songs that would be appropriate – as it was Harvest, traditional favourites such as *We plough the fields and scatter* (appropriate for a largely rural county such as Devon), but also more challenging words such as *Think of a world without any flowers*. The children chose some favourites too – *Christ be our light* in which the choristers always sing the descant even through they are mixed up with the whole school and it has not been practised! The final hymn was to be Marty Haugen's *Let us build a house* – very appropriate to the theme of homelessness and the shelterbox project. With a favourite *Gloria in Excelsis* and well-known *Sanctus*, most of the music was easily chosen. Some children prepared instrumental music to play before the service and as a reflection during communion.

Another group of children prepared the words to be used for the *Kyrie* Confession in the prayers of penitence and some intercessions including the response 'Gracious Lord, **shelter us with your love**'. The children collected their usual Harvest gifts, including toiletries and dry goods for a homeless project around the corner from the school, and made a huge display along one wall of the Chapter House. The art department and several children made a huge frieze that simply said 'Thank you' to place above it, and the school cook baked the bread that would be used for the Eucharist. A PowerPoint presentation of creation had been made for the separate Harvest celebration with the younger children (nursery to Year 2) designed as a back-drop to the preface and eucharistic prayer but it was decided that this probably detracted from the simplicity of the shelterbox theme so it was not repeated for this celebration – it is all too easy to have *too many* types of media used in a liturgy; sometimes simplicity is far better.

Presidential texts included the eucharistic prayer for which a special preface was written using words and images created by the children. The collect and the post communion were specially written in simple language to help all to pray together.

Because the Cathedral prepares children for Holy Communion before Confirmation and most of the 40 choristers take part in this each year, a large number of the school community receive Holy Communion. As is the school tradition, the children receive first followed by the staff and parents. Since the Eucharist is regularly celebrated, individual blessings are not offered except on Sundays; this does not feel unusual and, in any case, there is an acceptance that the school community is diverse and people are at different stages of their spiritual journeys – young and old – with different and with no faith at all.

The liturgy took well under an hour to celebrate, followed by tea and coffee for the staff and parents and play-time for the children. As is usual, the celebration involved a large number of adults and children working and praying together. The liturgy also has, in some senses, blurred boundaries – the preparation, the execution and the looking forwards all connect with the life of the school and the wider world and the liturgy is, therefore, seen as an integral part of the school community which also has blurred boundaries through the diverse families and communities that make it up.

The service

Rite: *Common Worship*: Holy Communion Order One (using the structure of A Service of the Word with a Celebration of Holy Communion)

Time: A weekday morning in the autumn term

Congregation: 120 children from years 3–8, 60 adults (staff and some parents)

Length of service: around 50 minutes

Musical resources: Piano, oboe, cello and flutes

Liturgical texts: A specially produced booklet was put together which included

- the words needed by the congregation
- rubrics (where needed)
- music for the *Gloria* and *Sanctus*
- illustrations (topical photographs and colourful graphics)

Examples of two pages from the service booklet are given here:

We thank thee then, O Father,
for all things bright and good,
the seed-time and the harvest,
our life, our health, our food.
Accept the gifts we offer
for all thy love imparts,
and, what thou most desirest,
our humble thankful hearts.
All good gifts...

Matthias Claudius 1740-1815, Tr. Jane Campbell 1817-78

SAYING SORRY

You have created a beautiful world which we have spoiled
Lord, have mercy.
Lord, have mercy.

You have supplied the world with enough food and water for
everyone, but it has not been shared out fairly.
Christ, have mercy.
Christ, have mercy.

You have given us gifts and talents which we don't always use.
Lord, have mercy.
Lord, have mercy.

The president says words of forgiveness

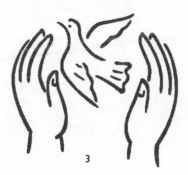

3

The Collect
a special prayer for the day is said

listen to a reading from the Bible
We share our thoughts and our stories

Hear the Gospel of our Lord Jesus Christ according to Luke
Glory to you, O Lord.

As they went on their way a man said to Jesus, "I will follow you wherever you go." Jesus said to him, "Foxes have holes, and birds have nests, but the Son of Man has no place to lie down and rest."

This is the Gospel of the Lord.
Praise to you, O Christ.

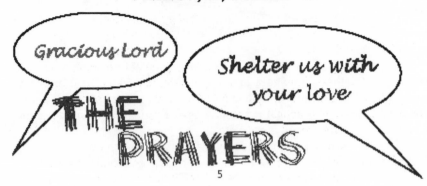

Gracious Lord

Shelter us with your love

THE PRAYERS

5

Holy Communion in a nursing home or hospital

Kate Lomax

The Revd Kate Lomax was until recently a Chaplain at the Cambridge University NHS Foundation Trust at Addenbrooke's Hospital. She has supplied the following notes on the background to this service.

Background

The opportunity of receiving communion for those facing illness in hospital is often gratefully received. Many patients, along with their families and friends, are actively seeking glimmers of God's grace in the midst of their difficulties. Holy Communion offers them the opportunity to encounter and experience that grace.

As with a great deal of worship with the sick, simple is best: the liturgy has in itself the potential to minister deeply to those present. Usually, the last thing patients and families want is a hymn marathon! Too much reading or singing can be exhausting. So it's worth keeping spoken words and hymns to a minimum and allowing worshippers to remain seated if this is more appropriate. In the setting of hospitals and nursing homes, familiar liturgy comes in to its own. Even those who are extremely ill, confused, or in the final stages of life can find comfort in familiar words. They can even drift in and out of them. I'm sure many of us will have experienced leading a service for the elderly in which a person who is apparently very confused and disconnected suddenly joins in with a familiar part of the liturgy held in their long-term memory. The use of prayers such as the Collect for Purity (a classic text, written on the hearts on many seasoned worshippers) will often strike a chord during such a service.

Because of this, it's perhaps best to see the liturgy as a gift and to avoid any temptation to be ultra creative. This being said, it is still possible to bring some creativity to bear on familiar texts and structures. A simple example is providing precious space for reflection by using music, art or silence. The use of multi-sensory worship ideas or rituals needs to be thought through carefully: the collective handling of objects can spread infection. Even communion wafers should be dipped into the wine before being eaten. However, with these limitations in mind, worshippers can always be given something to take away such as a prayer card and cross, or offered the chance to engage in practical ways perhaps by lighting a candle or attaching a prayer to a Prayer Tree.

Like many town centre churches, the chapel at the hospital where I worked stood on the 'high street' – in the hospital concourse, right next to the shops, the bank and the cafes. Because it is accessible and visible it is often a welcome sight to patients, families and staff. The services often attract people who wouldn't normally attend church but who, because of their situation, find themselves seeking God. The chaplaincy is ecumenical and therefore attracts people from a host of different churches and traditions. So sensitivity is required, and the need to discover, wherever possible, points of commonality. The chapel hosts a midweek and Sunday Eucharist. From there, many more patients throughout the hospital receive the Sacrament through the distribution of Holy Communion. Service cards are provided, the cards being laminated so that they can be wiped with antibacterial wash afterwards.

The example below took place on Palm Sunday. The liturgy was kept simple with only two hymns included. A period of reflection was kept between the readings and an uncomplicated ritual was used as an alternative to spoken intercessions. The style of the service was relaxed (a necessity, as people come in and out during the service) and gentle, with clear instructions to allow worshippers to engage fully and feel at ease.

The service

The service follows The Celebration of Holy Communion at Home or in Hospital (*Common Worship: Pastoral Services*, page 53)

¶ The Gathering

THE GREETING

The peace of the Lord be always with you.

PRAYER OF PREPARATION (Collect for Purity*)

HYMN: *Praise to the holiest in the height*

PRAYERS OF PENITENCE

The standard authorized text from CWPS, page 54, was used.

THE COLLECT

¶ The Liturgy of the Word

FIRST READING Isaiah 50.4-9a

REFLECTION

A CD track is played: 'Hope' from The Prayer Cycle *by Jonathan Elias.*[58]

GOSPEL READING Matthew 27.45-54

PRAYERS OF INTERCESSION

*A large plastic container (e. g. large bowl or dustbin) half full of water
is placed in the centre of the room. Each worshipper is given a stone
or pebble.*

*As each person holds their pebble ask them to imagine the worries and
cares that they carry (for themselves, their loved ones and the world).*

Space is given for reflection.

*Afterwards everyone is invited to drop the pebble into the water (either by
taking the pebble to the container or by having the container brought to
them) as a way of letting go of their concerns and giving them to God.*

¶ The Liturgy of the Sacrament

THE PEACE

A seasonal sentence is used to introduce the Peace.

*The exchanging of the Peace is kept to a minimum and expressed through
saying the response together.*

HYMN – *From heaven you came (The Servant King)*

PREPARATION OF THE TABLE

At the preparation of the table this prayer is said

> Pour upon the poverty of our love
> and the weakness of our praise
> the transforming fire of your presence.
> **Amen.**

CWPS, p. 56

THE EUCHARISTIC PRAYER (Prayer E)

The following preface was used

> It is right to give you thanks
> in sickness and in health,
> in suffering and in joy,
> through Christ our Saviour and our Redeemer,
> who as the Good Samaritan
> tends the wounds of body and spirit.
> He stands by us and pours out for our healing
> the oil of consolation and the wine of renewed hope,
> turning the darkness of our pain
> into the dawning light of his kingdom.
> And now we join with saints and angels
> for ever praising you and saying:

CWPS, p. 57

127

THE LORD'S PRAYER*

BREAKING OF THE BREAD

GIVING OF COMMUNION

> Jesus is the Lamb of God
> who takes away the sin of the world.
> Blessed are those who are called to his supper.
> **Lord, I am not worthy to receive you,**
> **but only say the word, and I shall be healed.**

CWPS, p. 60

PRAYER AFTER COMMUNION

> **Almighty God,**
> **we thank you for feeding us**
> **with the body and blood of your Son Jesus Christ.**
> **Through him we offer you our souls and bodies**
> **to be a living sacrifice.**
> **Strengthen us**
> **in the power of your Spirit**
> **to live and work**
> **to your praise and glory.**
> **Amen.**

Palm crosses are given out.

¶ Conclusion

A seasonal blessing is used as members of the congregation hold their palm crosses

> Christ crucified draw you to himself,
> to find in him a sure ground for faith,
> a firm support for hope,
> and the assurance of sins forgiven;
> and the blessing . . .

Note
* The Collect for Purity and The Lord's Prayer were said in traditional form on the grounds that this would be generally more familiar to a greater number of worshippers.

7

Case studies: *Christian Initiation* and *Pastoral Services*

The potential for flexibility contained within *Common Worship* is not restricted to regular eucharistic worship or to services of the word. Pastoral services – baptisms, marriages and funerals – so often lie at the cutting edge of our churches' mission and are an essential part of an Anglican understanding of community-based ministry. In these situations, where we are often conducting worship for those with little or no church background, there is a real need to be creative and to adapt material to suit personal circumstances. *Common Worship* helps this become a reality. The case studies in this chapter explore a number of possibilities within *Common Worship: Christian Initiation* and *Common Worship: Pastoral Services.*

- Baptism at a service of Holy Communion – Peter Moger

This example explores how a baptism dovetails with a celebration of Holy Communion. The service need not be over-wordy, nor over-long.

- Rites on the Way: Affirmation of Baptismal Faith – Anne Lowen

Among those finding faith today are both those with no Christian background and also those who wish to make a public declaration of faith as adults, having previously been baptized as infants. Anne Lowen discovers a resource which enables both groups to affirm their faith within in worship.

- Funeral Service using An Outline Order for Funerals – Peter Moger

The 'bespoke funeral' is a feature of the world we inhabit and is here to stay. With *Common Worship*, it is possible to create an individually tailored service without having to lose the essentials of a Christian funeral.

- The Marriage Service: Proper and special – Paul Bayes

Paul Bayes writes about the issues around the 'customization' of weddings and how making a marriage service 'special' can make all the difference, and be a genuine aid to mission.

Baptism at a service of Holy Communion

Peter Moger

Background and context

A couple of years ago, I was contacted by George, a recently priested curate who, in the absence of his incumbent, had been left to plan and preside at a baptism at a Sunday morning parish Communion. He had dutifully set out the service from CW Order One, and had then pasted in elements of the baptism service from *Common Worship: Christian Initiation.* George did a rough check of the timings for the service, panicked and phoned me, saying, 'I think it's going to last at least an hour and 40 minutes!' It would have done, had he included absolutely everything from Order One and the Baptism service. I suggested that he start again and, instead of asking 'What can I leave out of the service?' ask 'What needs to be included?' By using not Holy Communion Order One as his starting point, but A Service of the Word with a Celebration of Holy Communion, he was able to assemble an order of service that allowed for dignity and clarity, while being not over-wordy and contained within the hour.

The service below fell in the Epiphany season. Hence material from within the Seasonal Provisions (pages 150–65) in *Common Worship: Christian Initiation* was used, together with some texts from the Eucharist on the Festival of the Baptism of Christ from *Common Worship: Times and Seasons* (page 172). Advantage was taken of the recent amendments to the *Common Worship* baptism service, which allow the use of shorter alternative forms of the Decision (CWCI, page 168) and the Profession of Faith (page 178) 'where there are strong pastoral reasons'.

The service

¶ Preparation

HYMN – *Hail to the Lord's anointed*

THE GREETING

CWCI, p. 63

INTRODUCTION

> At our Lord's baptism in the river Jordan
> God showed himself to all who have eyes to see and ears
>   to hear.
> The Father spoke from heaven, the Spirit descended as a dove
> and Jesus was anointed with power from on high.
> Here is the door of faith,

through which we enter the kingdom of heaven.
As children of God, we are adopted as his sons and daughters,
and called out to proclaim the wonders of him
who called us out of darkness and into his marvellous light.

CWCI, p. 150

PRESENTATION OF THE CANDIDATES

CWCI, p. 66

This was moved to this earlier permitted position, thereby distributing the baptismal liturgy more evenly throughout the service and ensuring that the congregation was aware of the candidates at an early stage.

COLLECT

Heavenly Father,
at the Jordan you revealed Jesus as your Son:
may we recognize him as our Lord
and know ourselves to be your beloved children;
through Jesus Christ our Saviour.
Amen.

CWCPC, p. 14

¶ The Liturgy of the Word

GOSPEL READING Mark 1.4-11

SERMON

¶ The Liturgy of Baptism

THE DECISION

In baptism, God calls us out of darkness into his marvellous light.
To follow Christ means dying to sin and rising to new life with him.

Therefore I ask:

Do you turn to Christ?
I turn to Christ.

Do you repent of your sins?
I repent of my sins.

Do you renounce evil?
I renounce evil.

CWCI, p. 168

SIGNING WITH THE CROSS

CWCI, p. 68

SONG – *River, wash over me* (sung in procession to the Font) (CMP 581, SOF 487, TS 441)

PRAYER OVER THE WATER

Praise God who made heaven and earth,
who keeps his promise for ever.

Let us give thanks to the Lord our God.
It is right to give thanks and praise.

Father, for your gift of water in creation,
we give you thanks and praise.

For your Spirit, sweeping over the waters,
bringing light and life,
we give you thanks and praise.

For your Son Jesus Christ our Lord,
baptized in the river Jordan,
we give you thanks and praise.

For your new creation,
brought to birth by water and the Spirit,
we give you thanks and praise.

For your grace bestowed upon us your children,
washing away our sins,
we give you thanks and praise.

Father, accept our sacrifice of praise;
may your holy and life-giving Spirit
move upon these waters.
Lord, receive our prayer.

Restore through them the beauty of your creation,
and bring those who are baptized
to new birth in the family of your Church.
Lord, receive our prayer.

Drown sin in the waters of judgement,
anoint your children with power from on high,
and make them one with Christ
in the freedom of your kingdom.
Lord, receive our prayer.

For all might, majesty, dominion and power are yours,
now and for ever.
Alleluia. Amen.

CWCI, p. 153

PROFESSION OF FAITH

Let us affirm,
together with these who are being baptized,
our common faith in Jesus Christ.

Do you believe and trust in God the Father,
source of all being and life,
the one for whom we exist?
I believe and trust in him.

Do you believe and trust in God the Son,
who took our human nature,
died for us and rose again?
I believe and trust in him.

Do you believe and trust in God the Holy Spirit,
who gives life to the people of God
and makes Christ known in the world?
I believe and trust in him.

This is the faith of the Church.
This is our faith.
We believe and trust in one God,
Father, Son and Holy Spirit.

CWCI, p. 178

BAPTISM

CWCI, p. 71

THE WELCOME AND PEACE

CWCI, p. 75, 155

¶ The Liturgy of the Eucharist

This followed the Order for Holy Communion Order One (CWMV, pages 75–182), using some seasonal material.

HYMN – *In Christ alone my hope is found* (CMP 1072, SOF 1346, TS 1311)

PRAYER AT THE PREPARATION OF THE TABLE

> Open the heavens, Lord our God,
> and send your transforming Spirit
> on us and on these gifts.
> May we who are baptized into Christ
> be ready to share his cup of suffering
> and strengthened to serve him for ever.
> **Amen.**

CWT&S, p. 178

THE EUCHARISTIC PRAYER (Prayer H)

CWMV, p. 204

THE LORD'S PRAYER

BREAKING OF THE BREAD

GIVING OF COMMUNION

PRAYER AFTER COMMUNION

> Lord of all time and eternity,
> you opened the heavens and revealed yourself as Father
> in the baptism of Jesus your beloved Son:
> by the power of your Spirit
> complete the heavenly work of our rebirth
> through the waters of the new creation;
> through Jesus Christ our Lord.
> **Amen.**

CWT&S, p. 181

¶ The Sending Out

BLESSING

> God, who in his Christ gives us a spring of water
> welling up to eternal life,
> perfect in you the image of his glory;
> and the blessing of God almighty,
> the Father, the Son, and the Holy Spirit,
> be among you and remain with you always.
> **Amen.**

CWCI, p. 155

HYMN – *O breath of life, come sweeping through us* (CH4 595, CMP 488, CAHON 476, SOF 407, TS 379)

GIVING OF A LIGHTED CANDLE

CWCI, p. 77

DISMISSAL

CWCI, p. 77

Rites on the Way: Affirmation of Baptismal Faith

Anne Lowen

The Revd Anne Lowen is Assistant Chaplain at the Anglican Chaplaincy at Basle, Switzerland, in the Diocese in Europe. Anne has supplied the following notes on the background and context of the service.

Background and context

The Anglican Chaplaincy at Basle serves a large, international, multi-denominational, English-speaking congregation within the city. We do not own a church building so hold our two services each Sunday at two different locations. There is a traditional style evening service held in a small thirteenth-century chapel, and a mid-morning service in a modern building with a more informal, contemporary style of worship and children's ministry.

Julia is a single mother in her late thirties. She had attended church as a child but had fallen away as a teenager. She first came to our church a few years ago. She started attending more and more regularly and has developed a living faith. She had come to a point where she very much wanted to make some sort of public statement of her faith – to show how her life had been turned around and how she was making a fresh start with God. She had already been baptized as an infant and confirmed as a young teenager.

A total immersion baptism service for a mother, her ten-year-old daughter and a second adult had already been planned. It was suggested that Julia use this occasion for taking the public step she desired by reaffirming her baptismal vows, using the resources for the Affirmation of Baptismal Faith from *Common Worship: Christian Initiation* (page 197).

Julia really wanted this to be a fresh start and so, to prepare for the service, she requested a quiet service of the Reconciliation of a Penitent (*Common Worship: Christian Initiation*, page 273) before the main morning service.

The baptism took place in our more contemporary style service, which is held in a building with a purpose built pool for total immersion baptisms. However, practicalities in the layout of the church make the combination of using the pool for a baptism within a service of Holy Communion very complicated (if not dangerous!). The baptisms and Julia's Affirmation of Baptismal Faith, therefore, took place within A Service of the Word.

The service: Baptism by total immersion and Affirmation of Baptismal Faith within a Service of the Word

Page references are to *Common Worship: Christian Initiation*.

¶ Preparation

GREETING

p. 81

SONGS

INTRODUCTION TO THE SERVICE

The Liturgy of the Word

READINGS

SERMON

SONGS

The Liturgy of Baptism

PRESENTATION OF THE CANDIDATES

The candidates for baptism were presented using the form on page 84. The candidate for affirmation was presented using the form on page 200.

> *The president asks those affirming their faith*
>
> Julia, have you been baptized in the name of the Father, and of the Son, and of the Holy Spirit?
> **I have.**
>
> *The president asks the candidate*
>
> Julia, are you ready with your own mouth and from your own heart to affirm your faith in Jesus Christ?
> **I am.**
>
> *Testimony by the candidates may follow.*
>
> *The president addresses the whole congregation*
>
> People of God, will you uphold Julia in her life in Christ?
> **With the help of God, we will.**

THE DECISION (all candidates together)

p. 85/p. 201

SIGNING WITH THE CROSS (baptismal candidates only)

p. 86

PRAYER OVER THE WATER

p. 87

PROFESSION OF FAITH (all candidates with congregation)

p. 88/p. 202

BAPTISM

p. 89

Each candidate stepped into the pool separately for the liturgy of the baptism Following the baptism they then each sat at the side of the pool.

DECLARATION (affirmation candidate only)

pp. 203–4

This took place at the side of the pool, so as to avoid any confusion that it might in any way be interpreted as a 're-baptism'.
  The candidate for affirmation then entered the pool alone and immersed herself in the water, interpreting the rubric:

The candidates may come forwards to the font and sign themselves with water, or the president may sprinkle them.

pp. 203

SONG *(sung as the newly-baptized went to get dry)*

¶ **The Prayers**
PRAYERS OF INTERCESSION

THE COLLECT

THE LORD'S PRAYER

¶ **The Sending Out**

SONG

COMMISSION

p. 91

WELCOME

THE BLESSING

GIVING OF A LIGHTED CANDLE*

THE DISMISSAL

Note
* Julia brought hers which she still had from her infant baptism.

Funeral Service using An Outline Order for Funerals

Peter Moger

Context

Cynthia phoned me one day in the parish. 'You won't know me,' she said, 'but I'm dying and I'd like to talk with you about my death and plan my funeral. Actually, I'm a lapsed Roman Catholic, but I think I'd rather have a Church of England funeral. Is that OK?' We arranged to meet later that week. Cynthia was indeed dying – she had an aggressive form of cancer – and looked older than her 47 years. But her mind was sharp and her resolve was clear: 'I must get the funeral right.' Over the next few weeks we talked about life and death, about what Christians believe, and about how we might celebrate her life. She was an avid reader with a fine appreciation of the arts and of beautiful things: she loved poetry and music; she was an enthusiastic collector of shells. All these were important to her – and all had somehow to be included in the service.

The basic *Common Worship* Funeral Service would never have done Cynthia justice. But with the Outline Order of Funerals we had a structure which we could fill with content which both expressed the Christian hope and was personal to Cynthia. The congregation at the funeral was of mixed ages, but with 35–55 as the predominant age group. Most of these people – Cynthia's friends – were not churchgoers, but many spoke to me afterwards about the service. Two comments which were repeated were, 'We weren't expecting something like that!' and 'I'd like that sort of funeral myself.'

The service

Cynthia's coffin had already been brought into church. A large congregation was expected for the funeral – in the event somewhere between 300 and 400 attended – and so the family had requested some quiet time in church the evening before.

A large number of candles had been placed around the coffin. These were lit an hour or so before the start of the service.

As the members of the congregation arrived at the church they were each given a shell.

¶ The Gathering

The minister walked into church to quiet organ music.

The minister welcomed and greeted the congregation, introduced the service informally, and a short silence was kept.

Some sentences from Scripture were read.

'I am the resurrection and the life,' says the Lord. 'Those who believe in me, even though they die, will live, and everyone who lives and believes in me will never die.'

John 11.25,26

Blessed are those who mourn, for they will be comforted.

Matthew 5.4

God so loved the world that he gave his only Son, so that everyone who believes in him may not perish but may have eternal life.

John 3.16

Short tributes were made by Cynthia's husband, and by two close friends. During a piece of music, members of the congregation were invited to bring their shells forward and place them in front of the coffin in remembrance of Cynthia.

¶ Reflection, Reading and Sermon

Two poems – one of them written by Cynthia's 19-year-old son – were read.

A piece of music for reflection was played and the congregation was encouraged to spend time in reflection. The piece chosen, Arvo Pärt's Spiegel im Spiegel, *was one that had been particularly important to Cynthia. I had wondered about its suitability because of its length (well over 8 minutes!) but in the event, time seemed not to matter. (The undertakers had been warned to expect a funeral lasting around an hour!)*

Reading: Revelation 21.1-7

Sermon

Hymn – *Teach me, my God and King*

¶ Prayers

Prayers of Intercession

The Collect

The Lord's Prayer

¶ Commendation and Farewell

Cynthia was commended using the following set of words from Common Worship, *with her family standing around her coffin.*

Almighty God,
as you bring us face to face with our mortality,
we thank you for making each one of us in your own image
and giving us gifts in body, mind and spirit.
We thank you now as we honour the memory of Cynthia,
whom you gave to us and have taken away.
We entrust her to your mercy,
and pray that you will show us the path of life,
and the fullness of joy in your presence
through all eternity.
Amen.

CWPS, p. 374

¶ Dismissal

Blessing

The Committal took place at the crematorium.

The Marriage Service: Proper and special

Paul Bayes

The Revd Canon Paul Bayes is the National Mission and Evangelism Adviser, and since 2007 has been seconded part-time as a leader of The Weddings Project. He is an Honorary Canon of Worcester Cathedral. Prior to this, he has served as a Chaplain in Higher Education and as a parish priest in Oxford and Winchester Dioceses. Paul has supplied the following notes on the service.

Background

The Church of England's Weddings Project has conducted extensive research among couples and clergy to find out what leads people to choose a church wedding, and how to increase the numbers of those choosing church for their wedding and 'sticking' with the family of God afterwards.

What we found is that couples want the church service to be 'proper' – in other words they are delighted to share in worship that embodies and echoes the traditions of the Church. But they also ask that their service should be 'special', reflecting the words, music and ideas that matter to them. This is so important to couples that those who were able to make their service 'special' told us that they were more than three times as probable to engage actively with the church after the ceremony as those who were given no opportunity to customise their wedding.

So in talking the service over with couples, I have no difficulty in emphasizing and celebrating the legally necessary parts of the service, and in my experience couples don't have a problem with this either. The vows, the declarations, the Scripture reading – these are what make the service proper to the couple and their guests as well as to the Church.

And alongside that, I encourage a torrent of imagination and creativity in making the service unique to the couple – really, really special. Holding these things together needn't produce difficulty.

For example, if a couple asks for the opportunity to use vows that they've written themselves, I see that as an opportunity to listen, to discuss and then to offer – not to offer to scrap the legally necessary vows, but to offer any number of alternatives which catch the 'proper/special' partnership. So the couple can share the Church's liturgy, and then perhaps write down their meaningful promises and include them in the order of service, or choose or write an additional reading which catches the spirit of what they want to say to one another, or invite a moment of silence so that they can reflect together in the midst of their frantic day on what their marriage really means to them.

Like the liturgy itself, customization is a matter of word and action. It involves the choice of significant music, hymns and readings, but there's more. For example, one bridegroom had lost both his parents and the couple wanted to mark this in the ceremony. It was done unobtrusively by giving each guest a small bunch of carnations, tied with a ribbon bearing the parents' names, and inviting the guests to pray in silence as they held the flowers. The same groom said of his wedding 'I couldn't have asked for anything better.'

One last, important point. Customization can present clergy and church musicians with some stark choices between welcome and taste. Church professionals often have cultural preferences that differ from those of the popular majority, and unfortunately often the attitude of the Church to modern English culture is one of disdain. But of all the pastoral offices, weddings chime most with popular music and art. The lyrics and music of today's love songs speak deeply to the hearts of people at their weddings. And I suggest that one imperative on those of us who want to share in the mission of God is that we should practise the spiritual discipline of warmly welcoming cultural expressions with which we may have little personal resonance.

So welcome the couple – offer the proper liturgy they themselves are seeking – get creatively special – and don't despise the Spice Girls!

Wedding case study

Ben and Fiona chose to marry in their local parish church. Although neither of them was a regular churchgoer, both had had some contact with the church in the years leading up to the wedding: Fiona through her job as a teacher at the local primary school, and Ben as a representative of the local RAF Squadron. Fiona was also active in the town as a member of a dance group, and Ben was a member of the RAF station jazz band.

They were concerned that their wedding should be 'proper' in the sense that they wanted a 'traditional' service in church, but also 'special' – reflecting aspects of their personalities and their lives in the community. The vicar explained that, while certain aspects of the service were fixed, there was some scope for flexibility. Following discussion throughout the time of their marriage preparation, it was decided to explore the flexibility permitted around one particular area of the service – the Readings – thus allowing for the 'special' or 'customized' element alongside those parts of the service required by law.

¶ THE READINGS

1. Non-biblical Reading

Fiona and Ben had asked whether they might include a non-biblical reading, in addition to a reading from Scripture. With the vicar's help, they explored a number of possibilities and eventually chose to include Shakespeare's Sonnet 116:

> Let me not to the marriage of true minds
> Admit impediments. Love is not love

Which alters when it alteration finds,
Or bends with the remover to remove:
O, no! it is an ever-fixed mark,
That looks on tempests and is never shaken;
It is the star to every wandering bark,
Whose worth's unknown, although his height be taken.
Love's not Time's fool, though rosy lips and cheeks
Within his bending sickle's compass come;
Love alters not with his brief hours and weeks,
But bears it out even to the edge of doom.
If this be error and upon me proved,
I never writ, nor no man ever loved.

The reading – read by Fiona's brother – was printed in the congregation's Order of Service.

2.   Dance

This reading was followed by a dance created and performed by the local group of which Fiona was a member. The group had worked closely with the vicar in the weeks leading up to the wedding in order to make best use of the church building, the available space and the sound system. The choreography explored the theme 'two into one' and the dance was performed to a mixed sound track of popular and classical music assembled for the occasion.

3.   Biblical Reading – John 2.1-11

On the third day there was a wedding in Cana of Galilee, and the mother of Jesus was there. Jesus and his disciples had also been invited to the wedding. When the wine gave out, the mother of Jesus said to him, 'They have no wine.' And Jesus said to her, 'Woman, what concern is that to you and to me? My hour has not yet come.' His mother said to the servants, 'Do whatever he tells you.' Now standing there were six stone water-jars for the Jewish rites of purification, each holding twenty or thirty gallons. Jesus said to them, 'Fill the jars with water.' And they filled them up to the brim. He said to them, 'Now draw some out, and take it to the chief steward.' So they took it. When the steward tasted the water that had become wine, and did not know where it came from (though the servants who had drawn the water knew), the steward called the bridegroom and said to him, 'Everyone serves the good wine first, and then the inferior wine after the guests have become drunk. But you have kept the good wine until now.' Jesus did this, the first of his signs, in Cana of Galilee, and revealed his glory; and his disciples believed in him.

4.   Music

This Reading was followed by a musical item from Ben's RAF station jazz band. They wanted to play something which reflected Ben's great love of jazz, and yet which felt 'right' to be played in a church service. They came up with the idea of a movement 'In the beginning, God' from Duke Ellington's 'Sacred Concerts'.

5.   Address

In her address, the vicar brought together themes from the two readings, whilst also drawing on insights from both dance and jazz. In particular, she was able to focus on the creative tension which exists between careful choreography and freedom of expression in dance, and on the interplay of order and improvisation in jazz.

The result was that this part of the service enabled a high level of customization – elements which were 'special' for Ben and Fiona – as well as being firmly within the acceptable parameters of the *Common Worship* marriage liturgy. By including both dance and music within the Liturgy of the Word, it enabled a greater proportion of the congregation to engage with the content than might have been possible had there been only readings.

Conclusion

The case studies in this and the preceding two chapters have, I hope, shown that *Common Worship* offers us frameworks and resources which are flexible and which are able to sustain a healthy diversity in worship. This diversity is both exciting and a necessary part of what it means to be a vibrant, mixed-economy, missionary church.

Common Worship represents an enormous shift in our understanding of worship in the Church of England: of how it is constructed and resourced. Having lived for 450 years with a service book (or books) we are now in the situation where our common prayer as Anglicans is articulated very differently. We share common structures and certain key texts across our traditions and worshipping communities. But within those structures and supporting those key texts is an almost infinite bank of resources – authorized and commended – which is there to be used.

There is always the danger that, in planning worship, we choose to go for the 'low energy' option, the default setting, the basic format. This can, sadly, be seen in those churches whose services have changed very little, if at all, since the ASB was first authorized in 1980! While change for change's sake is never a good idea, we need to be asking continually whether our worship

- is the very best we can possibly offer to the God who deserves nothing less;
- helps all our worshippers meet with God and be open to his transforming grace;
- attracts and draws in those beyond the walls of the church community.

Planning vibrant, transformative worship is not easy. It requires vision and takes time and energy. But that time and energy are always well spent. Used creatively, *Common Worship* can help us fashion worship in ways that help our local churches encounter God and engage in our task of proclaiming afresh in each generation the faith of our Lord and Saviour Jesus Christ.

Appendix 1

The Canons of the Church of England which govern the liturgy used in public worship

B 1 Of conformity of worship

1. The following forms of service shall be authorized for use in the Church of England:

   (a) the forms of service contained in *The Book of Common Prayer;*
   (b) the shortened forms of Morning and Evening Prayer which were set out in the Schedule to the Act of Uniformity Amendment Act 1872;
   (c) the form of service authorized by Royal Warrant for use upon the anniversary of the day of the accession of the reigning Sovereign;
   (d) any form of service approved under Canon B 2 subject to any amendments so approved, to the extent permitted by such approval;
   (e) any form of service approved under Canon B 4 subject to any amendments so approved, to the extent permitted by such approval;
   (f) any form of service authorized by the archbishops under Canon B 5A, to the extent permitted by such authorization.

2. Every minister shall use only the forms of service authorized by this Canon, except so far as he may exercise the discretion permitted by Canon B 5. It is the minister's responsibility to have a good understanding of the forms of service used and he shall endeavour to ensure that the worship offered glorifies God and edifies the people.

3. In this Canon the expression 'form of service' shall be construed as including –

   (i)   the prayers known as Collects;
   (ii) the lessons designated in any Table of Lessons;
   (iii) any other matter to be used as part of a service;
   (iv) any Table of rules for regulating a service;
   (v)   any Table of Holy Days which expression includes 'A Table of all the Feasts' in *The Book of Common Prayer* and such other Days as shall be included in any Table approved by the General Synod.

B 2 Of the approval of forms of service

1. It shall be lawful for the General Synod:

    (a) to approve forms of services for use in the Church of England and to amend any form of service approved by the General Synod under this paragraph;

    (b) to approve the use of any such form of service for a limited period, or without limit of period;

    (c) to extend the period of use of any such form of service and to discontinue any such form of service;

and any form of service or amendment thereof approved by the General Synod under this paragraph shall be such as in the opinion of the General Synod is neither contrary to, nor indicative of any departure from, the doctrine of the Church of England in any essential matter.

2. Any approval, amendment, continuance or discontinuance of any form of service under paragraph 1 above shall not have effect unless the form of service or the amendment, continuance or discontinuance thereof is finally approved by the General Synod with a majority in each House thereof of not less than two-thirds of those present and voting.

2A. (1) It shall be lawful for the bishop of a diocese or other Ordinary of the place, on request made in accordance with sub-paragraphs (5) and (6) below on behalf of a parish or a place of worship of a kind specified in sub-paragraph (5) (a) below, by notice in writing to approve the continued use in the parish or place of worship, for such period as shall be specified in the notice, of any form of service –

    (a) the use of which has ceased to be approved by the General Synod by virtue of the expiry of any limited period imposed under paragraph 1 (b) above; or

    (b) the use of which has ceased to be approved by the General Synod by virtue of the expiry of any period of extension granted under paragraph 1 (c) above; or

    (c) which has been discontinued under paragraph 1 (c) above.

(2) Approval under sub-paragraph (1) above for the continued use of a form of service on a request made on behalf of a parish shall either –

    (a) apply to all places of worship in the parish in question; or

    (b) be limited in its application to such place or places of worship in the parish as may be specified in the notice.

(3) Where a bishop or other Ordinary has approved the continued use of a form of service under sub-paragraph (1) above he may, on a request made on behalf of the parish or place of worship concerned in accordance with

sub-paragraphs (5) and (7) below, by notice in writing extend (on one occasion only) the period of continued use of the form of service for such further period as shall be specified in the notice.

(4) The period of continued use referred to in sub-paragraphs (1) and (3) above shall commence on the date on which the use of the form of service in question ceases or ceased to be approved by the General Synod or on the expiry of the original period of continued use, as the case may be.

(5) A request for approval under sub-paragraph (1) above for the continued use of a form of service or for an extension under subparagraph (3) shall be made –

  (a) in the case of a place of worship which is in an extra-parochial place or in respect of which a clerk in holy orders is licensed under section 2 of the Extra-Parochial Ministry Measure 1967, by the minister concerned; and
  (b) in any other case, by the minister and parochial church council concerned acting jointly.

(6) A request for approval under sub-paragraph (1) above for the continued use of a form of service shall not be made after the expiry of the period of twelve months following the date on which the use of the form of service has ceased to be approved by the General Synod and the period for which approval is given shall not exceed three years.

(7) A request for an extension under sub-paragraph (3) above of a period of continued use for a further period shall not be made after the expiry of the original period and the further period shall not exceed the original period or two years, whichever is the less.

2B. (1) Paragraph 2A above (except sub-paragraphs (2) and (5) and with the omission from sub-paragraphs (1) and (3) of references to the Ordinary) shall apply to forms of service used in a cathedral church as it applies to forms of service used in a parish, with the following adaptations.

(2) Where Part I of the Cathedrals Measure 1999 applies in relation to the cathedral church, for references to a request on behalf of a parish or place of worship there shall be substituted references to the request of the Chapter with the consent of the dean.

(3) Where the Cathedrals Measure 1963 continues to apply in relation to a cathedral church in accordance with section 38 (3) of the said Measure of 1999, for references to a request on behalf of a parish or place of worship there shall be substituted references to the request of the following bodies acting jointly, namely –

  (a) the administrative body; and
  (b) the dean or provost as the case may be; and also
  (c) in the case of a parish church cathedral for the parish of which there is a parochial church council whose functions have not been transferred

to the administrative body in pursuance of a section 12 (1), that council. In this sub-paragraph 'administrative body' and 'parish church cathedral' have the same meaning as in the Cathedrals Measure 1963.

(4) In relation to the cathedral church of Christ in Oxford, for references to a request on behalf of a parish or place of worship there shall be substituted references to the request of the dean and Canons.

2C. In the case of a request in respect of a cathedral church or a place of worship which is in an extra-parochial place, the request shall only be made after consultation with the representatives of persons over the age of sixteen years who worship regularly therein.

3. In this Canon the expression 'form of service' has the same meaning as in Canon B 1 and the reference in paragraph 2A (5) (b) above to the minister shall, where there is no minister, be construed as a reference to the rural dean.

B 3 Of the form of service to be used where alternative forms are authorized

1. Decisions as to which of the forms of service authorized by Canon B 1, other than the services known as occasional offices, are to be used in any church in a parish or in any guild church shall be taken jointly by the minister and the parochial church council or, as the case may be, by the vicar of the guild church and the guild church council. In this Canon 'church' includes any building or part of a building licensed by the bishop for public worship according to the rites and ceremonies of the Church of England.

2. If there is disagreement as to which of the said forms of service are to be used in any such church, then, so long as the disagreement continues, the forms of service to be used in that church shall be those contained in *The Book of Common Prayer* unless other forms of service authorized by Canon B 1 were in regular use therein during at least two of the four years immediately preceding the date when the disagreement arose and the parochial church council or guild church council, as the case may be, resolves that those other forms of service shall be used either to the exclusion of, or in addition to, the forms of service contained in the said Book.

3. The foregoing paragraphs of this Canon shall not apply in relation to a cathedral which is a parish church nor to any part of a cathedral which is a parish church.

4. Where more than one form of any of the services known as occasional offices, other than the Order of Confirmation, is authorized by Canon B 1 for use on any occasion the decision as to which form of service is to be used shall be made by the minister who is to conduct the service, but if any of the

persons concerned objects beforehand to the use of the service selected by the minister and he and the minister cannot agree as to which form is to be used, the matter shall be referred to the bishop of the diocese for his decision.

5. Where more than one form of service of ordination of deacons or priests or of the ordination or consecration of a bishop is authorized by Canon B 1 for use, the decision as to which form of service is to be used shall be made by the bishop or archbishop, as the case may be, who is to conduct the service and, where more than one form of service of confirmation is so authorized, the decision as to which service is to be used shall be made by the bishop or archbishop, as the case may be, who is to conduct the service after consulting the minister of the church where the service is to be held.

6. In this Canon the expression 'form of service' has the same meaning as in Canon B 1.

B 4 Of forms of service approved by the Convocations, Archbishops or Ordinary for use on certain occasions

1. The Convocations of Canterbury and York may approve within their respective provinces forms of service for use in any cathedral or church or elsewhere on occasions for which no provision is made in *The Book of Common Prayer* or by the General Synod under Canon B 2, being forms of service which in both words and order are in their opinion reverent and seemly and neither contrary to, nor indicative of any departure from, the doctrine of the Church of England in any essential matter.

2. The archbishops may approve forms of service for use in any cathedral or church or elsewhere in the provinces of Canterbury and York on occasions for which no provision is made in *The Book of Common Prayer* or by the General Synod under Canon B 2 or by the Convocations under this Canon, being forms of service which in both words and order are in their opinion reverent and seemly and are neither contrary to, nor indicative of any departure from, the doctrine of the Church of England in any essential matter.

3. The Ordinary may approve forms of service for use in any cathedral or church or elsewhere in the diocese on occasion for which no provision is made in *The Book of Common Prayer* or by the General Synod under Canon B 2 or by the Convocation or archbishops under this Canon, being forms of service which in the opinion of the Ordinary in both words and order are reverent and seemly and are neither contrary to, nor indicative of any departure from, the doctrine of the Church of England in any essential matter.

4. In this Canon the expression 'form of service' has the same meaning as in Canon B 1.

B 5 Of the discretion of ministers in conduct of public prayer

1. The minister who is to conduct the service may in his discretion make and use variations which are not of substantial importance in any form of service authorized by Canon B 1 according to particular circumstances.

2. The minister having the cure of souls may on occasions for which no provision is made in *The Book of Common Prayer* or by the General Synod under Canon B 2 or by the Convocations, archbishops, or Ordinary under Canon B 4 use forms of service considered suitable by him for those occasions and may permit another minister to use the said forms of service.

3. All variations in forms of service and all forms of service used under this Canon shall be reverent and seemly and shall be neither contrary to, nor indicative of any departure from, the doctrine of the Church of England in any essential matter.

4. If any question is raised concerning the observance of the provisions of this Canon it may be referred to the bishop in order that he may give such pastoral guidance, advice or directions as he may think fit, but such reference shall be without prejudice to the matter in question being made the subject matter of proceedings under the Ecclesiastical Jurisdiction Measure 1963.

5. In this Canon the expression 'form of service' has the same meaning as in Canon B 1.

B 5A Of authorization of forms of service for experimental periods

1. Where a form of service has been prepared with a view to its submission to the General Synod for approval by the Synod under Canon B 2 the archbishops after consultation with the House of Bishops of the General Synod may, prior to that submission, authorize such form of service for experimental use for a period specified by them on such terms and in such places or parishes as they may designate.

2. Where any form of service has been authorized under paragraph 1 of this Canon for experimental use and it is proposed that it shall be used in any church the requirements of Canon B 3 shall apply.

3. In this Canon the expression 'form of service' has the same meaning as in Canon B 1.

The Canons of the Church of England, First edition 1969 (published by SPCK); Second edition 1975; Third edition 1981; Fourth edition 1986; Fifth edition 1993, incorporating two supplements 1998; Sixth edition 2000, First supplement 2005, Second supplement 2008; *Sixth edition* © *The Archbishops' Council 2000, Second supplement* © *The Archbishops' Council 2008.*

Appendix 2

Services authorized and commended

Authorized Services Alternative to the Book of Common Prayer as at 1 January 2009

Published in *Common Worship: Services and Prayers for the Church of England* and *Common Worship: Collects and Post Communions*

1   Calendar
2   A Service of the Word
3   Schedule of permitted variations to The *Book of Common Prayer* Orders for Morning and Evening Prayer where these occur in *Common Worship*
4   Prayers for Various Occasions
5   The Litany
6   Authorized Forms of Confession and Absolution
7   Creeds and Authorized Affirmations of Faith
8   The Lord's Prayer
9   The Order for the Celebration of Holy Communion also called The Eucharist and The Lord's Supper
10 Collects and Post Communions
11 Rules for Regulating Authorized Forms of Service
12 The Lectionary
13 Opening Canticles at Morning and Evening Prayer; Gospel Canticles; Other Canticles; A Song of Praise (Epiphany); Te Deum Laudamus

Published in *Common Worship: Christian Initiation*

14 Holy Baptism
15 Emergency Baptism
16 Holy Baptism and Confirmation
17 Seasonal Provisions and Supplementary Texts
18 Affirmation of Baptismal Faith
19 Reception into the Communion of the Church of England

Published in *Common Worship: Pastoral Services*

20 Wholeness and Healing
21 The Marriage Service with prayers and other resources
22 Thanksgiving for the Gift of a Child
23 The Funeral Service with prayers and other resources
24 Series One Solemnization of Matrimony
25 Series One Burial Services

Published in *Common Worship: Ordination Services*

26 Ordination Services

Published separately

27 Public Worship with Communion by Extension
    (NB explicit permission must be obtained from the bishop for the use of this rite.)
28 Weekday Lectionary

The above are all authorized by the General Synod for use until further resolution of the Synod.

Form of Service authorized by the Archbishops of Canterbury and York without time limit for use in their respective Provinces

A Service for Remembrance Sunday
(included in *Common Worship: Times and Seasons* – see below)

Commended Services and resources as at 1 January 2009

Published in *Common Worship: Services and Prayers for the Church of England*

1 Introduction to Morning and Evening Prayer on Sunday
2 Introduction to Holy Baptism
3 Short Prefaces for the Sundays before Lent and after Trinity
4 Additional Canticles

Published in the President's Edition of *Common Worship*

5 Additional Blessings

Published in *Common Worship: Christian Initiation*

6 Rites Supporting Disciples on the Way of Christ
7 Admission of the Baptized to Communion

8   Celebration after an Initiation Service outside the Parish
9   Thanksgiving for Holy Baptism
10 A Corporate Service of Penitence
11 The Reconciliation of a Penitent

Published in *Common Worship: Pastoral Services*

12 An Order for Prayer and Dedication after a Civil Marriage
13 Thanksgiving for Marriage
14 Ministry at the Time of Death
15 Receiving the Coffin at Church before the Funeral
16 Funeral of a Child: Outline Orders and Resources
17 At Home after the Funeral
18 Memorial Services: Outline Orders and Sample Services
19 Prayers for Use with the Dying and at Funeral and Memorial Services
20 Canticles for Marriages, Funerals and Memorial Services

Published separately

21 Material contained in *New Patterns for Worship*
22 Material contained in *Common Worship: Times and Seasons*
23 Material contained in *Common Worship: Festivals*

Services which comply with the provisions of A Service of the Word (see Authorized Services, no. 2) as at 1 January 2009

Published in *Common Worship: Services and Prayers for the Church of England*

1   An Order for Morning Prayer on Sunday
2   An Order for Evening Prayer on Sunday
3   An Order for Night Prayer (Compline)
4   An Order for Night Prayer (Compline) in Traditional Language

Published separately

5   Sample services contained in *New Patterns for Worship*
6   Services contained in *Common Worship: Daily Prayer*

Publications

The material is published in the following volumes:

- *Common Worship: Services and Prayers for the Church of England*
- *Common Worship: President's Edition*
- *Common Worship: Collects and Post Communions*

- *Common Worship: Christian Initiation*
- *Common Worship: Pastoral Services*
- *Common Worship: Daily Prayer*
- *Common Worship: Times and Seasons*
- *Common Worship: Festivals*
- *Common Worship: Ordination Services* (Study Edition)
- *New Patterns for Worship*
- *Public Worship with Communion by Extension*
- annual editions of the *Common Worship* Lectionary

It may also be found in the *Common Worship* area of the Church of England web site.

Versions of the Bible and of the Psalms

The following may be used in *Book of Common Prayer* services (with the permission of the Parochial Church Council) instead of the Authorized Version of the Bible and the Psalter in *The Book of Common Prayer*:

- Revised Version
- Jerusalem Bible
- Revised Standard Version
- Good News Bible
- New English Bible (Today's English Version)
- The Revised Psalter
- The Liturgical Psalter (The Psalms in a new translation for worship)

Any version of the Bible or Psalter not prohibited by lawful authority may be used with Alternative Services and Commended Services.

Appendix 3

The ordering of worship in fresh expressions of church under Bishops' Mission Orders

Extracts from the Code of Practice for the Dioceses, Pastoral and Mission Measure 2007

'In the worship of God the full meaning and beauty of our humanity is consummated and our lives are opened to the promise God makes for all creation – to transform and renew it in love and goodness.'[59]

The ordering of common worship is a vital part of the life of any Christian community. The worship of God is central to the life of His Church. Worship is a means by which the Christian community is enabled to respond to God's grace, is sustained in a life of discipleship and is connected to the wider Body of Christ.

There is a need for the whole Church to continue to reflect on its patterns of worship, particularly in respect of fresh expressions of church and mission initiatives as these develop and grow. This work is currently being taken forwards in a dialogue between the Liturgical Commission and the Archbishops' initiative, *Fresh Expressions*, who will together develop more comprehensive guidance in due course. This appendix consciously builds on the section on worship in fresh expressions of church in the report *Mission-shaped Church*.[60]

1 Two principles

1.1 The creative dialogue between context and tradition

The working definition of a fresh expression of church quoted in para 4.1.5 of this Code indicates that a fresh expression of church will be shaped in its growth to maturity on the one hand by the Gospel and the enduring marks of the Church and on the other by its cultural context.

This creative dialogue between context and tradition is likely to be seen most clearly in the ordering of worship. On the one hand the context may call for different approaches to worship in (for example) a community of parents and young children; a group of teenagers; a small house fellowship;

or a group of older people meeting midweek. On the other hand, the common Christian tradition calls for some common elements in that shaping in order to preserve connection and unity within the Body of Christ.

1.2 The journey and formation of the Christian community in worship

Many fresh expressions of church take as their starting point in worship points of familiarity to those they are seeking to serve. A new midweek congregation serving the elderly may begin with the Book of Common Prayer. An all-age after-school gathering may begin with a 'shape' that is more like a school assembly. A deanery youth congregation may adopt the styles and patterns of a larger Christian festival within a particular tradition.

However, each fresh expression of church will find itself in the early years of its life on a journey to growth and maturity. These years are therefore probably to be a period of formation and change and will entail experiment and reflection as a new community engages with its context, finds faith together and engages creatively with different parts of the Christian tradition.

2 Public prayer and the administration of the sacraments

Christian worship has, from the beginning, had a dimension which is public and one which is domestic and centred on the homes of Christian people (Acts 2.46; 20.20).

Although some principles for the ordering of Christian worship apply to every context, the Church of England's Declaration of Assent makes it clear that there is a particular need for good order and accountability in public prayer and in the administration of the sacraments.[61] S 47(4) of the Measure, which deals with the provision to be made in a Bishop's Mission Order for the administration of the sacraments, serves to confirm that this must be in accordance with the legal rules applying in the Church of England as a whole. (See also paras 5.4.1–10 of this Code.)

In some cases, the life of a fresh expression of church begins in a home or another private context and does not involve the administration of the sacraments. An example might include a network of cells meeting across a benefice, with each member also attending a Eucharist regularly in one of the parish churches. The ordering of non-sacramental worship in such a context is not prescribed or limited by the Canons of the Church of England, and the use of authorized liturgy is not required.

When worship is conducted in public, or when it involves the administration of the sacraments (whether in public or in private), however, attention needs to be paid to the relevant legal requirements (including Measures and Canons) and to the authorized liturgy.

3 The relevant Canons

The attention of those responsible for worship in mission initiatives governed by a Bishop's Mission Order is drawn to Canons B 1 to B 5A of the Canons of the Church of England, which deal with the forms of service authorized or allowed by canon law (including the *Common Worship* services referred to in paragraphs 4.1–3 below), and also the 'ecumenical canons', Canons B 43 and B 44. (Both of these have been amended by Amending Canon No 27 which accompanied the Measure, to deal specifically with Bishops' Mission Orders. See also paras 4.5.3–13 of this Code and Appendix 1 Part C).

Canon B 5 permits the minister conducting a service to 'make and use variations which are not of substantial importance' in authorized forms of service. In addition, Canon B 4 permits the Archbishops or the Bishop to approve forms of service for use on occasions for which no other provision is made, while Canon B 5 allows a minister having the cure of souls[62] to use or permit the use of forms of service which he or she considers suitable on such occasions. In all these cases, the variations or form of service must be 'reverent and seemly' and 'neither contrary to, nor indicative of any departure from, the doctrine of the Church of England in any essential matter'. If any question is raised concerning the observance of Canon B 5, it may be referred to the Bishop 'in order that he may give such pastoral guidance, advice or directions as he may think fit'.

Canon B 3 deals with decisions as to which of the authorized services are to be used. Where the decision relates to a service (other than the occasional offices) in a church or building licensed for public worship, it is to be taken jointly by the incumbent and the parochial church council. Where an initiative under a Bishop's Mission Order holds services elsewhere, these will be subject to the provisions of Order itself; it is good practice for decisions about the ordering of worship to be taken collaboratively by those authorized to lead the initiative together with a representative group from the community, and the forms of worship should be kept under regular review.

4 Provision in *Common Worship*

4.1 A Service of the Word

A Service of the Word (*Common Worship*, pages 19–27) provides a minimal outline structure for developing worship in a fresh expression of church. *New Patterns for Worship* (Church House Publishing, 2002) offers an abundance of particular resources and texts for use within that structure. Texts for use at most points in the service may also be devised locally.

4.2 A Service of the Word with Holy Communion

In the administration of the sacraments, the orders of service authorized and allowed by canon are of necessity somewhat more restricted than for the

Service of the Word, but A Service of the Word with Holy Communion (*Common Worship*, page 25) provides a framework which none the less offers considerable flexibility.

4.3 Services of Initiation

The authorized liturgies for baptism, confirmation and affirmation of baptismal faith are published in *Common Worship: Christian Initiation* (2006), together with 'Rites on the Way' for use with those preparing for Christian initiation. Particular attention should be paid to the notes and rubrics in the Baptism service – not least to identify those parts of the service that may be either omitted or paraphrased.

5 The authorization and training of ministers

Where there is appropriately such variety in forms of worship and an expectation of continuous reflection, development and journey, it is vital that careful attention is paid to initial and continuing training and formation in liturgy for those called to lead worship in fresh expressions of church.

6 The role of the Visitor in the development of worship

As with every part of the Visitor's work, this dialogue about the development of worship within the framework set by the Canons and *Common Worship* should be conducted in a context of mutual trust and respect and a desire to strike the most helpful balance between the needs of the mission context and the riches of the tradition at this particular point in the journey of the community.

Notes

1 *Transforming Worship: Living the New Creation*, a report to the General Synod by the Liturgical Commission, 2007, p. 1.

2 Rowan Williams in an interview for BBC local radio, March 2008, quoted at www.freshexpressions.org.uk/section.asp?id=1378

3 A helpful summary of this work is given in R. C. D. Jasper and P. F. Bradshaw, *A Companion to the Alternative Service Book*, SPCK, 1986, pp. 23–8.

4 Philip Tovey, *Mapping Common Worship*, Grove Worship Series, number W 195, Grove Books, 2008.

5 www.cofe.anglican.org/worship/liturgy/texts

6 www.vislit.com

7 CWMV, p. ix.

8 *The Renewal of Common Prayer: Unity and Diversity in Church of England Worship*, Church House Publishing/SPCK, 1993.

9 *The Renewal of Common Prayer*, p. 90.

10 ' "If the law supposes that," said Mr. Bumble, "the law is a ass – a idiot. If that's the eye of the law, the law is a bachelor; and the worst I wish the law is that his eye may be opened by experience – by experience." ' Charles Dickens, *Oliver Twist*, chapter 51, first published serially 1837–39.

11 See TW 2.12.

12 *The Canons of the Church of England*, 6th edition, Church House Publishing, 2008.

13 www.cofe.anglican.org/about/churchlawlegis/Canons

14 *Common Worship: Times and Seasons*, pp. 573–85.

15 General Synod, *Report of Proceedings*, February 2007.

16 www.cofe.anglican.org/worship/liturgy/commonworship/texts/newpatterns/notes/planninghc.html.

17 This may be obtained by email from ccu@c-of-e.org.uk

18 Appendix 3 to Part V of the Dioceses, Pastoral and Mission Measure 2007, reproduced as Appendix 3 on page 158, available to download at: www.cofe.anglican.org/about/churchcommissioners/pastoralandclosed churches/pastoral/mission/bmos/bmocode.doc

19 Declaration of Assent, *Common Worship MV*, p. xi.

20 See: http://www.cofe.anglican.org/info/yearreview/dec07/ churchwedding.html

21 Though ministers should be aware of Canon B 20.3, which reminds of the need to check the appropriateness of words and music sung in worship.

22 www.cofe.anglican.org/worship/liturgy/commonworship/texts

23 *Together for a Season: Seasonal Resources for All-age Worship*, ed. Gill Ambrose, 3 volumes, Church House Publishing, 2006, 2007, 2009.

24 www.chpublishing.co.uk/product.asp?id=2392142

25 *Faith in the City: A Call for Action by Church and Nation*, Church House Publishing, 1985, 6.110.

26 www.cofe.anglican.org/worship/liturgy/commonworship/texts/word/ sotw.html

27 www.cofe.anglican.org/worship/liturgy/commonworship/texts/word/ sotw.html

28 www.cofe.anglican.org/worship/liturgy/commonworship/texts/funeral/ funeral.html#outline

29 Peter Craig-Wild, *Tools for Transformation: Making Worship Work*, Darton, Longman & Todd, 2002.

30 Sue Wallace, *Multi-sensory . . .* series, Scripture Union, 2000–.

31 *Together for a Season*, ed. Gill Ambrose, 3 volumes, Church House Publishing, 2006–2009.

32 CWT&S, pp. 226–9.

33 The full order of service may be found in *Together for a Season* volume 2, Church House Publishing, 2008, pp. 20–31.

34 *Sing God's Glory*, Canterbury Press, 2001.

35 Available to members and affiliated churches. See www.rscm.com/ publications/sbys.php

36 *Sunday by Sunday for the Second Service Lectionary*, RSCM / Canterbury Press, 2008.

37 www.cofe.anglican.org/worship/liturgy/commonworship/texts/collects/
collectsfront.html

38 CWMV, note 5, p. 375.

39 CWMV, pp. 21–3, 26–7.

40 Introduction to ASOTW, CWMV, p. 21.

41 *Psalm Praise*, CPAS, 1973.

42 *Psalms for Today* and *Songs from the Psalms*, Hodder & Stoughton, 1990.

43 Anne Harrison, *Recovering the Lord's Song: Getting Sung Scripture back into Worship*, Grove Worship Series W198, Grove Books, 2009.

44 www.cofe.anglican.org/worship/liturgy/commonworship/texts/daily/
canticles

45 CWMV, note 8, p. 27.

46 CWT&S, pp. 439–40.

47 From CCLI: www.ccli.co.uk

48 The Invitation to Confession is taken from the 1984 Service for Remembrance Sunday, as reproduced in *Common Worship: Times and Seasons*, copyright © The Archbishops' Council 2006. The Confession is adapted from a text in *For the sake of Justice* (Churches National Housing Coalition 1995) see Churches National Housing Coalition/Housing Justice, www.housingjustice.org.uk. The Blessing is based on a prayer by Janet Morley from *All Desires Known*, © Janet Morley, 1992 (expanded). Other material is taken from *Common Worship: Services and Prayers for the Church of England*, copyright © The Archbishops' Council 2000–2008.

49 Tim Lomax and Michael Moynagh, *Liquid Worship*, Grove Worship Series W 181, Grove Books, 2004, p. 3.

50 *All-age Everything*, Kevin Mayhew, 2001, revised edition, 2009, copyright © Nick Harding, 2001, 2009 reproduced by permission.

51 Gill Ambrose, Peter Craig-Wild, Diane Craven and Peter Moger, *Together for a Season: Lent, Holy Week, Easter*, Church House Publishing, 2007, p. 188.

52 Simon Parry, 'God you're so cool', copyright © 2003 Vineyard Songs, 252 Cottingham Rd, Hull HU6 8QA.

53 Administered by worshiptogether.com songs excl. UK and Europe. Administered by kingswaysongs.com: www.kingsway.co.uk. Used by permission.

54 www.messychurch.org.uk

55 www.freshexpressions.org.uk/dvd

56 *Messy Church: Fresh Ideas for Building a Christ-centred Community*, Barnabas, 2006.

57 The service is adapted from Lucy Moore, *Messy Church 2*, BRF, 2008, used by permission.

58 Jonathan Elias, *The Prayer Cycle*, copyright © 1999 Sony Music.

59 *Common Worship*, Preface, p. ix.

60 *Patterns of Worship*, MSC, p. 117.

61 The Declaration of Assent is prescribed by Canon Law and made by all ordained ministers. In the context of affirming the faith professed by the Church of England, the minister declares that 'in public prayer and the administration of the sacraments I will use only the forms of service which are authorized or allowed by Canon'.

62 An incumbent or priest in charge will fall within this category, as will some team vicars and assistant curates.